I0566584

MINDS

@

WORK

4

MINDS

@

WORK

4

First Step
Publishing
Paving Ways For New Writers

First Published in India in 2015 by First Step Publishing
Editorial / Sales / Marketing Office at
303-304 Garnet Nirmal Lifestyles Ph 2
Behind Nirmal Lifestyles Mall
LBS Marg Mulund West
Mumbai 400080
E-Mail:- info@firststepcorp.com
www.firststepcorp.com

Copyright © Authors Copyright

All rights reserved. No part of this publication may be
reproduced, stored in or introduced into retrieval system
or transmitted in any form or by any means
(electronically, mechanically, photocopying, recording or
otherwise) without the prior written permission of the
publisher . Any person who does an unauthorized act in
relation to this publication may be liable to criminal
prosecution and civil claims for damages.

ISBN: - 978-93-83306-31-2
Publisher: First Step Publishing
Branding, Marketing and Promotions by: Design Fishing
Digital Management by: First Step Corp
Cover Design: Design Fishing
Typeset in Book Antique
India Paperback: ₹ 299
Rest Paperback: $ 8

Sr No	Author Name	Page No
1	Arna Sarka	6
2	Ibironke Oluwatobi	9
3	Purba Chakraborty	15
4	Iram Fatima Ashi	24
5	Debasish Mishra	28
6	Surbhi Thukral	41
7	Barkha Parikh	45
8	Lovita J R Morang	48
9	Heena Ahuja	76
10	Anuja Bhatia	79
11	Divya Bandodkar	83
12	Rohan Acharya	95
13	Satyananda Sarangi	98
14	Dr Waseem Malla	102
15	Susmit Sarkar	106

Arna Sarka

Arna Sarka; currently a student of Comparative Literature, Jadavpur University, Kolkata is also a chess player. She has received The Telegraph Excellence Award for her performances in chess. She claims to be in love with poetry and likes reading story books. Apart from writing and chess, her interest lies in painting and making portraits.

She.

Smile, her smile is all I like
Eyes, her eyes shines like dew drops on my mind.

She is so divine, she is so free...
I am so afraid- she might flee
Like the fresh spring's refreshness
That is how she sews her grace
Like the violets against the sky
She just perfectly walks by
And her soul is so so pure
That even the most scarlet sins, gets washed for sure

Lovely as such is her face
That even the moon fails its pace
With all the virtues in the world
Mother nature created her with ardent heart.

My train journey.

In my childhood train journey
I would wait for a tunnel to come my way
Till it comes I would pray
And when it came
I would dance its gay
I never wondered when it would end
My happiness too would never faint
For maybe I knew, I knew it then
My helpless mind would always gain
So the tunnel would come again.

But now I don't know what happened.
I think of the- after tunnel's end.
And then my joy comes to fail-
I forgot the track of my rail. . .

I like my childhood, childhood train.
I like its rainbow. I like it's rain.

Ibironke Oluwatobi

Ibironke Oluwatobi is a young writer. He has several published poems and articles on social topics. He is currently a member of the Orientation Broadcasting Service (O.B.S) team of the National Youth Service Corps (NYSC). He lives in Lagos, Nigeria.

Give Me Eden

Every drop of blood is borne out of one man's evil
When hate simulates smiles
And forgiveness becomes extinct
I beg my imagination
To give me Eden

Every time the pen meets the paper
It draws a picture of elegy
Holocaust and savagery
Boils the temperature of peace
Take this molten ambience of the world
And give me Eden

Every time the eye sees the picture
My countenance falls sick
Sorrow leaves nothing to be happy about
And everything to pour sorry on
I miss the verdant origin of man
Give me Eden

Nothing To Trust

Journeying from Elysium
The big blue marble introduced me to the society
Where mothers are sorry for the birth of their daughters
And fathers compete with their sons
Friends' list having false heading
We call ourselves brothers
but trust is the nub
We were born equal
Till success started drawing histograms

Now, I'm coming of age
yet my peer group is empty
The society you turn to seek answers,
asks further questions
In there, pressure keeps climbing atmospheres
melting down unacquired innocence
Vision blurred by ladies with their ups and downs
In prayer we shut our eyes
but the munificence of a moonlighter illuminates us
That's norm trying to influence our impression
Perplexing us with the gaudiness of pleasure

There is politics without principle
Pleasure without conscience
Wealth without work
Knowledge without character
Methods without morality
I see humans without humanity
A culture of unkind mankind

My patience is warning your anger
The man with the handkerchief desires to fetch your tears
It is already a cold city,
Why gather cool friends?
A place where you hold the key,
But to a faulty lock
Turning everyone to an opportunist
Chances are disguised,
Opportunities are poisoned
There is nothing to trust

Umbrellas Won't Stop The Rain

The wind that approaches is gruff
Look as it swings the tree tops to vagaries
And tears down the leaves of summer
Foundations we trusted, yanked by its whirl
It pours the sea vehemently to the shores
The breeze is absent to it mop back
I can't feel the warmth of a while ago
It disappeared like the ghost of forget

I listen with a heart fit to break
As thunder ceaselessly strikes the floating clouds
Causing it to pour down its burden
Surely, our session of laboured bliss is disturbed
No one came with shoes to dance,
Everyone wears a common desultory
The badly off are besieged by the cold
Noble men aim for their siege-mentality cloak

Do not be helped to the wrong shelter
Be cautious of the hoax
Offering Umbrellas in fair weather
To repossess it when the drops begin
Our thirst for showers is clearly hidden
In a pale and drought skin
We should not wait for the rain to have fallen
And in *faulte* de *miuex*, fetch from the flood

Let's not forget the inspiration of the torrent
How seasonal it falls

13

To later rise like aired balloon forming the body of the
sky
Leave me to sweat in the rain
Till it obeys me as it sires to gravity
Let me stand in it
Stretching out my mettle
To pick the best of the rainbow's colours
Umbrellas won't stop this rain
It's just a license to bear under it.

Purba Chakraborty

Purba Chakraborty is the author of "Walking in the streets of love and destiny" (2012) and "The Hidden Letters" (2014). She is also a web content developer, a blogger and a singer in leisure. Many of her poetries, short stories and articles have been published in several anthologies and magazines such as Rhymes and Rhythm, Melange ~ a potpourri of thoughts, Stories for your Valentine and Fusion: a mingled flavor mocktail. She is currently working on her next manuscript. She derives equal amount of pleasure in writing prose and poetry. She basically lives to write and writes to live. She is a keen and empathetic observer, which helps her to conjure tales and verses on paper. Life and Nature are her source of daily inspiration. When she is not writing, she is either lost in books or music.

Rose, the painter's beloved!

It was a ritual for Mr. And Mrs. Datta to visit the Academy of Fine Arts every Sunday. Their irrevocable love for arts managed to metamorphose their arranged marriage into a romantic one. After all, the earth transforms into Arcadia when we meet someone with whom we share an object of passion. In their case, it was definitely arts.

Both of them were professors in the Presidency College of Kolkata. They spend their hours of leisure marveling at the unique collection of paintings in their home. They seldom missed attending any reputed painting exhibitions, despite their hectic schedules. According to them, an ideal life meant peaceful hours with your life partner in the company of arts and music.

The Saturday Newspaper read:

A Vintage World at the Academy of Fine Arts: Drop in to see the collection of prime and classic paintings collected over the period of time. Paintings are for sale too.

As Mrs. Datta read the piece of news, she was instantly lured by it and programmed her mind to buy the most beautiful vintage painting from the exhibition. When she shared the idea with her husband, he found it fascinating too.

"But the vintage painting will make a deep hole in my pocket," He said, as an afterthought.

"If they are too much costly, we won't buy, but at least, we can look at the range of paintings tomorrow." Mrs. Datta said in a dismal manner.

***

The couple strolled around the huge hall which was embellished by some of the finest paintings of the world. On reaching the extreme corner of the hall, they were enticed by a composition. Unlike the other artworks which they came across some minutes before, this was comparatively simple yet bewitching.

It was a colorful portrait of a beautiful damsel. The colleen had eyes that spoke a thousand tales of lesions and agonies yet her blood red lips carried a subtle heart melting smile. Her hair was uncombed and bedraggled, which magnified the grace of the painting. The tangles in her hair resembled the knots and complexities of her mind. The painting seemed so real.

The bottom right corner of the painting was, however, crumpled and had burning marks which reached till the damsel's lips.

"Do you think this burning effect was made by the artist to enhance the delicacy of the painting?" Mrs. Datta spoke with reverence.

"Must be. Had it been a real fire, it would have burned the entire creation. The fire wouldn't have cleverly stopped just beneath the lips." Mr. Datta justified.

"You are wrong. The burning marks are the result of the fire. It is no coloring effect." An eavesdropper interrupted the couple, to their sheer annoyance.

Mrs. Datta smiled meekly whereas Mr. Datta could not conceal his vexation.

"Pardon me for interrupting. I am Nibaran Mallik, a researcher of ancient art and culture. This painting

17

known as Rose was created by David Eugene. A lot has been written about this painting.

"Is it the painting of the artist's beloved?" Mrs. Datta could not hide her inquisitiveness.

"The artist fell in love with the lady in this painting after creating her. It's written in a few books that the painter embraced and loved this lady like a human till the day he died. Even on his death bed, this painting was with him."

"Intriguing." Mr. Datta said, furrowing his eyebrows.

"Please tell us more about the painter and this painting, if you can spare some time." Mrs. Datta pleaded to the researcher's delight. He started narrating after clearing his throat.

"It was the time of the late 1950s. David Eugene was fifty-five then, tormented by poverty and loss of his family. Though he was a very skillful painter and his works were appreciated by all, earning a living solely by this skill was tough. He fed his wife and son through his skill graciously, but an act of God turned his world upside down.

A massive and disastrous tsunami drowned his home and killed his family. Not only did he lose his family but also his money, expensive paints and brushes, some of his masterpiece works and the purpose of living. It's said that nothing is really lost until you lose your purpose of living. The once acclaimed painter was then a lonely soul, seeking for company and tranquillity.

He tried to bond with the clouds, the flowers, and the birds, but the hollowness within him refused to ebb down. He painted beautiful landscapes and sold them for one rupee in the nearby market. The scanty sum of money could hardly feed him a few grains. He tried to save from that little amount to buy colors and brushes.

His poor and haggard appearance repelled people from him and he was caged in his small hut. Only Nature seemed to have mercy as it did not abandon him. On one winter day, he was enthralled to find fresh red roses on the other side of the road. He sat a few hand distance from the shrubs and started captivating the marvelous beauty of nature in his canvas. The flowers were transformed so beautifully and aesthetically on paper that the painting got sold on a higher rate than usual.

He was happier than the other days because he understood that his art has not forsaken him. However, a vacuum engulfed him as soon as he reached his hut. The dark interior with only a flickering candle resembled the darkness of his life. With bountiful tears, he went to sleep every night. That night was dangerously different. An inexplicable urge to love someone and to talk to someone conquered his soul. He wanted company desperately. After tossing and turning for an hour, he got up.

He lighted a candle and clipped a fresh new paper on the cardboard. He wanted to transcend his longing, desires and fantasy on the paper. He started with a woman's hair and made it charcoal black, long and lustrous. However, he did not want to make it straight and arranged. He incorporated several meshes and made the hair fall all over the place. It was as if the woman is struggling with her hair in a stormy night. David tangled her hair to portray his complicated relationship with the woman. He moved a little below and started drawing the eyes. He drew her eyeballs in the leftmost corner of each eye which made it appear that the woman is looking at the painter from the corner of her eyes. The kohl under each eye was smudged revealing the fact that she has cried profusely.

When David breathed life into her eyes and dipped them with torment and agony, his eyes watered too. Actually in his mind, he tried to establish a relationship with the lady in the painting. He considered the painting to be living and the lady to be his beloved, the only one he has on the planet. The reason for ingraining the woman's eyes with uncountable sorrows was the complicated love shared between this woman and the painter.

He drew the nose and outlined the lips with the same passion. As he tried to color the lips, he noticed that the red color tube had no color left in it. A feeling of despondency and frustration occupied his soul. In a jiffy, he slit his left index finger with a blade kept aside. A fountain of blood oozed out from the deep slit.

David soaked the paintbrush in his fresh, clear blood and filled the lips of the damsel following the outline made by the pencil. The lips were slightly pouted out and did not carry any smile. David looked at the damsel in incredulity. It was not an ordinary painting for him; it was his life. It seemed that he had found a mate in his lonely, secluded life.

He named the woman Rose. Rose looked so lively and effervescent that David started telling her his worries, woes and agonies without hesitation. He was happy because Rose has a part of him in hers; his blood is also the kernel of her existence.

It was the crack of dawn and a pulchritudinous Rose was born. David was madly in love with her. The more he adorned his creation, the more he fell in love with her. He knew that he created Rose with smiles and tears on his face and ecstasy, woe, angst and love in his heart. His emotions, his blood, and his soul are now a part of Rose.

"Who says we can only love the so-called mortals? We can love anyone and anything we share our emotions and soul with." David said in his soliloquy.

David thought that it was the time to tell Rose about his love for her. He gazed at Rose, who looked at him in anticipation. "I am in love with you, Rose. You are my beloved. From now onwards, you are also my life. Even if I perish, I will be alive within you. Do you love me too?" David looked at the lady for a few minutes, but no reply came, obviously.

Pangs of hopelessness pricked his mind and he thought how insane he was to ask such a question to a painting. His reverie was interrupted by a faint burning smell. He was shocked to find that the candle which was kept a few inches below the canvas has led to a catastrophe.

His newly made work, his beloved Rose was almost on the verge of turning into ashes. David hooted in pain and trepidation as he saw the fire reaching Rose rapidly. He was numb with helplessness. As the fire was about to burn Rose's beautiful lips, David saw a slight movement in the lady's lips. He rubbed his eyes and found that the fire was retreating back steadily.

The lips of the lady twitched extremely slowly and her lips miraculously curved to produce a smile. David was bewildered with the miracle and fainted. When he woke up, he saw that the smile still lingered on Rose's lips. He was convinced that his Rose has a life.

Till the day David died, his world revolved around Rose. There was a deep, unbreakable bond between the mortal David and the immortal Rose. When David was about to take his last breath, he whispered to Rose, his beloved, "Be mine forever my love, even after my death. Don't be someone else's." These were the last parting words of David."

Nibaran Mallik completed the story and smiled. Mr. and Mrs. Datta looked at him speechless, deciding whether they should believe in the tale.

"I want this painting." Mrs. Datta exclaimed, after a few minutes silence.

"This painting does not stay in anyone's house for more than two days." Mallik grinned.

"Why? It is such a marvelous work with a great history. " Mr. Datta enquired.

"The last words of David to Rose were: Be mine forever. So whoever takes this painting in his or her home cannot keep it for long." Mallik replied.

"I don't believe such things. The story behind the painting was indeed intriguing, but this painting is a painting. It is not a person that it will run away from someone's home." Mr. Datta retorted.

"They, why couldn't it stay in anyone's home till date? More than a hundred people have purchased this painting, just to return it after a few days." Mallik asked.

Mr. and Mrs. Datta did not reply to his question. They looked at each other for a while and decided to ignore the words of Nibaran Mallik. They happily purchased the vintage painting without a second thought. The couple came home, happy and proud of their purchase. They settled Rose on the wall of their living room and looked at the painting with a smile of contentment.

They called all their friends and invited them in the next weekend to their house so that they could flaunt the vintage painting which had a fascinating history.

***

The next morning as Mrs. Datta woke up and walked to the living room, she was terrified. She screamed loudly, which woke up her husband.

"What's wrong, my dear?" Mr. Datta came running to her.

"Look!" Mrs. Datta pointed her finger at the painting.

The lady in the newly purchased painting looked different. The smile on her lips was replaced by a frown.

The couple gazed at each other, with shivers running down their spine.

Iram Fatima 'Ashi'

Iram Fatima 'Ashi', is a nonresident Indian staying in Saudi Arabia. Born and raised in India she has lived in different places and explored different people and their cultures. Though connected by her soul she msses India.

Travelling has been an important part of her life. She has always felt as though borders are just the constructs of our feeble intellects, we have to look beyond them, only then will our hearts be free. After spending so many years in different cultures and places, her quest is far from over. She wants to travel till her last breath and she feels that she doesn't belong to any particular culture. Iram Fatima have accepted whole world as her own and have a deep desire to be buried wherever she dies.

Acadamically she has pursued graduation and post graduation in English and has been writing since the age of 13 in Hindi, Urdu and English. Currently working as an Editor in chief of 'Reflection online magazine', Editorial Executive Sub-Committee member of VIEW (Print journal) and her creative work is part of 22 international anthologies. Her articles, short stories and poems are published in Indian magazines and newspapers. Internationally, her work is also published in Canada and US.

She feels blessed on being honored by 'achievement award' in India by Aagman group on 19th July 2015.

Her hobbies include reading, writing, painting, listening to music and observing nature and she takes inspiration from real life, nature and anything which touches her.

She is a poetess, writer, painter and overall an artist by heart.

Her poems and stories are simple yet subtle. You don't need much literary prowess to understand its depth.

Happy Reading...

Love

Iram Fatima 'Ashi'

O' my life

A climb on mountain, to discover peak of height,
A glimpse of thunder, to witness its spark of light,
A flight, to discover all fascinating shades of sky,
Still to be done, so bless me more time, O' my life.
A kiss to milky cloud, to check its softness and moist,
A scream in valley, to check echo that never voiced,
A gentle hold on flower, to see beauty and to feel
rejoiced,
Still to be done, so bless me with time, O' my life.
Few more dances are left to attempt in rain shower, to
enjoy,
I want to splash water from river by throwing stone as
toy,
Want to lie down whole day on grass to feel calm and
joy,
Still to be done, so bless me with time, O' my life.
I want to wake up to sunrays and live in shiny
moonshine,
A swim to see the depth of sea and collect treasure of
mine,
I want to fly with wild air and challenge the storm,
Still to be done, so bless me with time, O' my life.
I was rushing for things, which belongs to worldly line,
Taking this life as internal, didn't value precious time,
So many things to finish, before I lose my life's rhyme,
Now desirous to complete, so bless me with time, O' my
life.

How can I be with you?

Wandering in cold darkness,
Lost all hopes and desires,
Want to end this dead journey,
Why do you still want me with you?

I bore a lot, without letting out a sigh
Never demanded or complained,
You were always in my heart and soul,
Did you ever wish me in your prayers?

You were amazed when I loved you,
You froze, when I was leaving you,
You didn't even utter a word to stop me,
In all those years, have you ever missed me?

Now you want me to come back,
Accepting all your faults, for my love,
Want to pay me back in happiness,
With nothing left inside, tell me how can I trust?

Have always loved you more than myself,
But now I have aged and withered
My lackluster looks please none
When I'm gone, will my absence be missed?

Debasish Mishra

Debasish Mishra, a native of a small town in Odisha called Bhawanipatna, derives immense pleasure from writing. Since his childhood, his ink is his sole solace. He equally enjoys writing poems and stories. He is the recipient of the Poesis Award of Excellence For Literature. His ink has featured in nationwide magazines like Competition Success Review, Competition Refresher, GK Refresher, GK Today, Ravenshavian and Utkal Bharati. Academically, he has won the inaugural Brindavan Mishra memorial award for being the best student of his district in 2006, by securing the 9th rank in the +2 arts stream of CHSE, Odisha.

His poems/stories have been published in various anthologies. An ex-banker, he resigned from service to devote more time to literature.

The Other Side of Love

"Your attention please, train no. 12306, New Delhi-Howrah Rajdhani express, is running late by one hour and fifty-five minutes. The inconvenience caused is deeply regretted."

Ananya looked into her watch with utter desperation and slammed her fist on the cemented pedestal. The huddle of men around her – comprising of coolies, ticket collectors, fatigued travellers, reluctant onlookers, desperate vendors and many more – was sickening. Most of them would covetously stare at her as they passed on the platform. She hated crowds and the deafening din that followed. The sweltering summer added insult to injury. The effluence of sweat tried to relegate her beauty by washing away the copious make-up, which she had smeared on her skin for this special occasion. All the embellishment - the glossy lips, the kohl-clad-eyes, the cheeks painted with a tinge of orange and the silky unbraided hair - was meant for that special person, Shabbir Khan.

***

A year ago, Ananya was pursuing her masters in Delhi University. She first saw Shabbir in a social gathering where she had befriended Rhea. This tall and stout fellow, donned in a black blazer over a pink shirt, was the cynosure of the night. He flaunted a clean-shaved dusky face, excepting the dark lined moustache that stretched above the lips and dripped on both sides, almost forming a semi-rectangle. His brown eyes had a certain kind of eloquence. Rhea whispered in the ears of her friend, "See that handsome hunk. Doesn't he look like Ajay Devgn?"

Ananya smiled or rather blushed. She was obviously attracted to this young man, who had some similarities with her favourite actor.

"Who is he? What does he do?" she asked.

"His name is Shabbir. Shabbir Khan. He is a young tycoon", replied Rhea.

Ananya was thinking of all kinds of ideas to walk to him and start an interaction.

"Hello, sir. I am Ananya Chakraborty. I have heard a lot about you. It's a pleasure to meet you here", she nervously rehearsed, chanting the words to herself.

Nonetheless, the shy side of her nature suppressed the spontaneous impulse. Before she could overcome her coyness, the dashing young man had disappeared.

Fortunately, for Ananya, she met him again. This time, the venue was Nizamuddin railway station. Ananya had been there to see off her closest chum, Rhea. Without wasting any time, she rushed to him and said, "Hi, sir. I am Ananya Chakraborty. I have heard a lot about you. I last saw you in a social gathering. Before I could walk to you, you had disappeared..."

Shabbir smiled genially. Ananya felt relaxed for pouring out the emotions, which were turbulently popping in her interior ever since she saw him.

"Nice meeting you, Ananya. What do you do?" he asked.

"I am pursuing my post graduation in Delhi University."

"That is really nice. I always respect a woman of substance."

"I am a body of lesser mettle when compared to you, sir."

"Don't call me sir, please. It makes me feel I am old", he joked.

"What shall I call you then?"

"Shabbir. Only Shabbir".

"Okay, Sir".

Shabbir responded with an irate stare and then burst into laughter. Ananya joined him too.

After a few minutes of silence, Ananya asked, "What are you doing here? Waiting for somebody?"

"No. I am actually waiting for my train. I will go to Vishakapatnam for a friend's wedding".

"But you could have taken the aerial route."

"See, Ananya. I enjoy train journeys. When there is no urgency, why should I fly and lose these thirty hours of memorable moments?"

Ananya was deeply touched by his philosophies.

"Despite being an affluent tycoon, he is down-to-earth and humble", she thought.

"Can I have your number?" she asked candidly, breaking all cannons of shyness.

"Yeah, sure".

Shabbir dictated the number and Ananya saved it in her phone book. Without any demand from Shabbir, she dialled a missed call and childishly remarked, "It's my number."

Shabbir smiled. Ananya smiled again.

Meanwhile, the train to Vishakapatnam arrived. Shabbir entered into his compartment (a general sleeper coach). As the train left the station, leaving behind a gust of smokes and a foul smell, Ananya waved her hands frantically. Shabbir craned his neck through the door and displayed a prophetic smile as usual. The duo looked at each other, as long as their faces were visible. Gradually, distance separated the two.

"Are mere Jhansi ki rani. Your confidence and candour are commendable. This is a different Ananya", Rhea winked at her.

She was kept on the sidelines for a long time, ever since Shabbir came into the picture.

Ananya blushed. Soon the train, for which Rhea had been waiting, arrived, and Ananya retreated to her hostel.

A small matchstick can burn an entire forest. Similarly, this one incident opened up new chapters in the life of Ananya. Frequent phone calls, messages and clandestine meetings followed. Ananya was rechristened as 'Annie' and Shabbir was called 'Shona'. Their intimacy escalated with every passing day. On one occasion, while the duo were in a coffee shop, Shabbir kneeled before Ananya in a melodramatic manner, kissed the backside of her palm and embellished her finger with a ring. A diamond ring.

Then he declared in a loud voice, "Ladies and gentleman, I am madly in love with this special person. I want to marry her. And if she agrees, all your bills will be paid by me".

The people around them clapped their hands. A few young guys, probably college students, clicked photographs furtively and shouted, "Please say 'yes', bhabiji".

Ananya was taken aback. She was waiting for this moment. But when it actually happened, it seemed surreal. It was a tough surprise to digest. Nevertheless, she reined her raging emotions, tried to appear normal and replied, "I love you too... equally, if not more".

The crowd exulted rapturously, as though India had won the cricket world cup. Shabbir and Ananya looked into each other and conversed with the silent language of love.

Then, there were promises for a lifetime alliance and unflinching togetherness. Social barriers tried to thwart their bond.

"How can you marry him? Apart from being a Muslim, he lacks a family. He looks like a traitor. I cannot allow this marital alliance", her father grunted loudly.

"I love him. And it is the only thing that matters in any relationship. Had looks and religion been the recipe for a happy marriage, such squabbles and tussles would not have proliferated in between mama and you, and she would not have faced an untimely death!" she retorted aggressively.

Her father was diffident, almost uncompromising. She was obstinate. The deadlock divided the father and daughter, who were till now inseparable. Her father had been her friend and guardian ever since the abrupt departure of her mother. But time is gravid with shocks and surprises.

Despite the differences, Ananya decided to marry Shabbir. This new relationship was legitimized through a court marriage. It was followed by a solemn ceremony with limited guests, solely from Shabbir's background. Soon after the alliance, Shabbir flew to Dubai for a business assignment. However, Ananya chose to stay in a rented flat in Kolkata, which comprised of a bedroom, a hall, a kitchen and a toilet. The locality was not a preferable one, but her purpose was to educate the little kids residing around her. The windows ushered in the sordid smell of urine whenever she hoped to welcome some light into the dark rooms. The wall below served as an ageless toilet for the vendors of the market and the other passersby who crossed the place with brimming bladders. Despite complaints and requests, the ritual of lowering the trousers and splashing the wall continued. The discomfort of the area faded with the solace that she elicited through the smiles in the faces of the helpless kids whom she taught. Moreover, she had learnt the art of acceptance from Shabbir.

After a year of separation, she was waiting for him with unbridled enthusiasm in Kolkata, where he was expected to arrive shortly. He would attend a brief session with his partners and stakeholders in Delhi and then come to Kolkata in a train because of his affinity to train journeys. "Affluence should never erode the essence and joys of amusement", he often said.
***
The extra couple of hours passed with impatience and desperation for Ananya. Finally, Rajdhani express

arrived. From the huddle of passengers, the countenance of Shabbir emerged, like the flash of the moon amid countless stars. She welcomed him with wistful eyes. He reciprocated with similar feelings. Without a second thought, she pounced on him and hugged him tightly as though they were separated for ages. It was an emotional reunion of two parted souls, the joy of first rainfall in a parched place after months of scorching summer.

Together, they proceeded to the stinking flat, hand in hand, soul in soul.

"When will you go?" she asked.

"Next week", he replied.

"Why did you come then?"

"Ohho. I will come back soon. These are unavoidable errands. Otherwise, you know well that you are my first priority."

She looked angry. To pacify her, he leaned towards her body, kissed her lips and whispered in her ears, "Hope Annie understands that Shona loves her dearly".

Cleaving through the anger, a curve appeared in the lips of the damsel. She kissed him back more intensely. The night marked the culmination of their love.

Shabbir had been to the market to buy green vegetables. It was a rare privilege for Ananya. She laughed at the very thought that a renowned business tycoon was bargaining in the market for a rupee or two, solely on her instructions. Meanwhile, she was unpacking the bag of her spouse, taking out the official documents and the clothes. All of a sudden, her eyes fell on a small diary. She opened it with curiosity and scrolled through the pages. On the very first page, some names were scribbled, and alongside, the contact numbers were noted. There was also a map of India in the end of the diary with red dots marked on it. The other pages abounded in code words. She was perplexed. She could not understand anything. She looked at the names yet again, which appeared in the first page - Abu Qasim, Jehan Rahman, Mohammad Rafiq and others.

She googled the names, one by one, and observed that all these persons were accused in various bomb blasts throughout the country. Then, she reanalyzed the map again and observed that the marked dots were actually the places, which had been wrecked by bomb blasts. Her hands trembled nervously. She sweated profusely. Wrinkles of concern emerged in her countenance.

"It might just be a coincidence. Those accused in the bomb blasts may not be the same persons whose names are written in the diary. The duplicity of names is a possibility", she consoled herself, in a bid to counter the growing scepticism. The doorbell jangled. Ananya nervously tucked the diary below her bed, wore an expression of normalcy, and opened the door. Shabbir was standing helplessly with two overloaded bags while the tail of a gigantic fish stemmed out from one of them. She took the bags from his hands with a smile, a fake smile.

"I never knew vegetables are this expensive", he chuckled, looking at the red imprints that the heavy bags had stamped on his fingers.

"I am going for a bath", he announced after some time and entered into the bathroom. Ananya shrewdly seized the opportunity. His mobile phone was lying in the table.

She had never intruded into his privacy before. But now, she, like a sleuth, skimmed through the messages, the emails, the call records and the other sources of data. She found a message from an unknown number, sent a few months ago, which read: "Blast successful as per plan." Prior to it, Shabbir had texted, "Money sent. Results awaited." She was shocked and scandalized. Tears emanated from her tender eyes. Maybe, she regretted her decision to marry a man, who funded terrorist blasts in various parts of the country.

That very evening, she eavesdropped to a conversation where her husband directed someone to infuse suicide bombers in the crowded markets of Kolkata.
"This city is a soft target. I will send the money tomorrow. Peel it off its grandeur", he muttered with a cocky grin. She was broken, yet helpless. With judiciousness and sagacity, she decided to embrace silence and feigned ignorance.

While she was chopping the vegetables in the evening, Shabbir walked to her. He clasped her from behind and whispered slowly in her ears,
"Dear Annie. I know very well that you have taken my diary. It has important contacts and information. Please return it to me".
"Which diary?" Ananya retorted back nervously as if she did not know anything.
"Ohho. Don't act innocent. I know everything. I am also aware that you surreptitiously eavesdropped to my phone conversations."

Ananya swallowed a lump, garnered some fortitude, and said, "It's okay if you cheated me. But why did you cheat my country?"

"Hey", shouted Shabbir with a frightening glare, "your country has cheated me".

"What are you saying? Is not it your country?"

"It was my country. It is not, anymore. When I wanted to start a business, I ran from office to office, bank to bank. The government did not heed my wants. My parents died because of them. But these people helped me... They identified my skills, invested in me, and made me a businessman. Now it's my turn to return their services".

"They used you, dammit".

"I love you Ananya. But don't test my loyalty. Give the diary".

A brief scuffle resulted. Ananya obdurately denied handing over the diary. In a fit of fury and desperation, Shabbir ransacked the almirahs, the tables, the several racks of books and periodicals, and finally found the diary from beneath her bed. She tried to stop him.

"I will not stay here for a moment more", he yelled insolently.

This other side of her spouse - the darker one - vexed her.

Before he could exit the flat, she, in utter desperation, picked the knife from the tray of chopped vegetables and shoved it into his belly. A stream of blood rushed from his body. Her eyes poured copious tears in response.

A few minutes later, she mustered some courage and ringed her father.

"Why have you called me?" her father asked tersely.

She remained quiet as though she was also dead along with Shabbir, whose corpse lay before her like a statue of her sacrifice.

"Is everything alright?" the wizened man - who melted within no time - queried with ample concern.

"You were right. He was not a good match", she blurted.

"What are you saying, Anu?"

"Yeah, papa...And hence I have killed him."

"W-h-a-t? Are you crazy? You loved him."

"I still love him...but I love my country more! And he was a terrorist."

Soon tears covered her countenance.

Suddenly, she wiped her tears, burst into a strange kind of laughter, fluttered the bloodstained knife before herself, and bellowed, "Yes, I have killed him."

Bewildered, her father said, "I am not able to understand you, beta. Wait for me. I will reach your place within no time. Don't do anything silly." There was no response from Ananya's end.

A spell of silence lingered like the quietude after the storm....while the concerned father kept on shouting desperately, "Anu...Anu....Answer me....Where have you gone? I am reaching within no time... Anu..Anu....!"

That Inquisition

Today I remember
Your flurry of questions
I clearly realize
The reason of that inquisition
As to what I would do
When you would desert me?

I fatuously giggled
At that point of time
Deeming it an impossibility
Or rather, a humorous statement.

But now as I stand
In the mid of this solitude,
Enveloped by darkness and melancholy,
Flicking my tears by myself,
That agonizing enquiry
Reverberates in the interior
Flaring a myriad tempests
In the emptiness of my heart.

Surbhi Thukral

Surbhi Thukral is a new mother of a beautiful boy. Apart from being a doting mother, she writes fiction and poetry. She holds Masters in Business & Management from the University of Strathclyde, UK. She can be reached at thukral.surbhi@gmail.com

Her work has been published in the Harvests of New Millennium, EWR: Short Stories, Taj Mahal Review, A World Rediscovered (An Anthology of Contemporary Verse), eFiction India, The Indian Trumpet, 2013 New Asian Writing Short Story Anthology, Minds@ Work 2, Seasons of Love, Fusion — A Mingled Flavour Mocktail, The Orange Frame Literary Review, Her Story: Is Not Always a Story, Upper Cut: A Change India Initiative, Miles Apart: An Anthology, All About My Name Poetry Series by Silver Birch Press, Rhymes and Rhythm and Story Mirror.

Do You Remember?

Do you remember the sweet taste of snow
Upon it we strolled arm in arm
And the moon melted upon our hearts?
Do you remember the kiss
I planted upon your lips?
Do you remember my touch on you,
The love making, our hearts entwined?
Do you remember the longing in our eyes
Even before the goodbyes?
Do you remember that evening?
It was soaked in the fragrance of lilac.

In My Dreams

In my dreams, my existence lives
Between the breath of words,
My poetry adorns sagas of glory,
And my prose kisses the palm of sun,
In my dreams, I see gilded days and nights,
Summers and winters embrace
The depth of my heart,
My dreams make me feel alive
Albeit my damned life.

Tonight

Tonight, the gentle breeze hums a sweet melody,
The silvery moonlight performs a ballet
Upon the waves of the sea,
Drops of rain glisten as precious gems
In the pages of my diary,
See the sky pour shimmer of gold upon
My fate lapped with years soaked in tears,
Tonight, my dreams glow with the fire of stars,
Embrace the vastness of sky and depth of the sea,
Tonight, my dreams fly like the untamed wind.

Barkha Parikh

Barkha Parikh is an I.T. engineer and also a Computer teacher from Ahmedabad, Gujarat. She is an avid reader and can hog books just like cup cakes. She can read any genre at any time. She writes for a Cause and Not for an Applause and the cause is – ' To touch many hearts and Enlighten many souls." She pens down whatever her heart feels. She believes in 'Live in Present because Present means a Gift'. She is a bubbly , Full-of-Life girl but at the same time too emotional. She loves spreading smiles. Her only mantra in life is – "I romance words, I write." There had been a time when she had no one to listen to her and she got confined to a shell. But today she has more than 64000 readers on her blog who listen to what her heart says. She is a Cold-Coffee addict and to know her more visit her blog – U, Me n Coffeetalks (http://coffeetalkwithbarkha.blogspot.in/). She made her debut with a book – "Minds @ Work 2" which is an anthology of poems. Her story "A Dollop of Romance" is also published in an anthology – "Drenched souls". She has also made a remarkable contribution in great anthologies like "Minds @ Work 3", "Blank Spaces", "Purple Hues" and "The Fallen Angels".

MY SILENCE SCREAMS ~ Barkha Parikh

The Words all I had seemed to fade…
And the silence of my soul bayed…
I looked for them with a torch in the dark…
Neither a ray of them was seen nor a spark…
I dug down to the silt…
And discovered, they had gone with a jilt…
Half-buried in the slime…
I found them with a sound of chime…
Letters after letters I arranged them right…
To my surprise the word formed was "W.R.I.T.E."
Now through this word, My Silence Screams…
With no noise made by Broken Heart and Shattered
Dreams!

Lovita J R Morang

Lovita J R Morang is a professional filmmaker, artiste, and poet.

Green Oscar entrant acclaimed film "Discovery of Rhododendron Forest-where highest Rhododendron grows, Eastern Himalayas" is the first film on Rhododendron Forest. She has seventeen books-Anthologies published internationally. And represented her works on international and National film/literary festivals .She has twenty-one books-Anthologies of poetries and short stories that she shared with renowned Poets of India and the world. Her book "Discovery of Rhododendron Forest of Eastern Himalayas-an encyclopaedia" is a prestigious book.

She started filmmaking early at the age of Twenty. And have made more than Twenty Documentaries, travelogue, tele-films. She has acted in a number of movies and TV serials. Casted as a princess in a docu-drama on massacre of Royal dynasty of Nepal,produced by BBC Channel, London directed by Clive, 2005 as Protogonist for Sundance Award Winner Sandhiya Sundaram's short celluloid Cinema-DOREMIFA, and - "Echo-Rongkuchak" National Award for Student and Best film in Vienna Film Festival by Dominique produced by FTII,Pune and Satyajit Ray Film Institute,Kolkatta. Among many TV serials, she is the protogonist for Sahitya Academy Award Winner Writers Sayed Abdul Mallick directed by Gauri Burman and Rita Chaudhury in 13-episode serial directed by national Award winner, Gautam Bora and Chaurav Chaliha directed by Kaushik Nath. A graduate from Girls' Handique College and Guwahati University, short-term course on film appreciation from FTII, Pune.

Represented as a speaker:

1. On the Sports Scenario and technology India at Olympic Meet,Spain in Bangalore.
2. World Grassroot's Comic Society,Canada in Guwahati.
3. Delhi Poetry Festival.
4. Kumaon Literary Festival, founder Suman Batra,Chaired Barka Dutt,Journalist,NDTV.

She is involved presently in research and study of climate indicator wildflowers from Eastern Himalaya and feels the urgent need to conserve hundred of Rhododendrons and new recorded species and trying best to keep her passion for writing.

I didn't kill her
-Confession of an AA

I didn't kill her…. I didn't kill her….

Recounts Sobetso Kri.

The light from the bulb, hanging from the ceiling illuminates the dark shades on his face, by the dominant wavelengths of lights. That eliminates, furthers the doubts to decide that something in actuality went wrong. He couldn't restrain the guilt, the serious injury caused by him. He had killed somebody, not sure enough but absorbed in thoughts, the intensity of purpose itself driving him to find the purpose. The inner circumspection's desire to reach for equitable elucidation. Suddenly, a saintly concern, in virtuous beneficence, the dichotomized version of a twofold occurrence like that of both celestial as well as earthly joy, mythicized. Like the bad housing of the best cities, like the milk and blood that flows out of temples. Recurring in scattered instances not occurring in expected times.

Time doesn't allow. It's hard, honestly for people to keep secret. Why is it so hard to keep a secret? The basic instinct is true instinct. The gut feelings are sporadic. Like the nesting place on highest of the cliff, any bird can reach for. Like the secret hard to serrate. It seems the natural feelings are nature's good times, uncorrupted.

What did I kill?

Mosquitoes, Cockroaches, rats and being hunted the animals illegally he killed….images of various things capriciously juxtaposed in his mind. Yet, undecided. Impulsive. Unpredictable.

Predictably, these are the living things he often killed and would confess with pride, how many mosquitoes or rats he had killed. He would lay the dead bodies in an array. Then he would call everyone to see. He derived joy.

This joy was detested by Rosenlu.

He recalls....

"Killing anything is killing," she would acquaint with.

"And the amount of blood these mosquitoes sucks, our grandpa died of Malaria, so no mercy. And you want me to let it all go. Overlook things that spread epidemic, clarifies Sobetso but all terminate into tragic upshot of all surfacing infectious diseases, like itchy eczema on skin was the cruel conversation inside, gives rise to fear, anxiety, anxiety disorder, illness unidentified but felt bottomless.

"Higher suicides in depressed women," Sobetso reads out, that was written in the newspaper used for wrapping the orange squash bottle, which he brought from the daily bazaar, Tezu.

"Don't talk like a genetically gifted grieving monster," said Rosenlu in a low-pitched tone.

"Listen to what tissues from the brain can talk minute written here in this piece of paper...

Females with depression have abnormally high expression levels of many genes that regulate the glutamate system, which is widely distributed in the brain. Glutamate is the major excitatory neurotransmitter in the brain. Schizophrenia, epilepsy, autism and Alzheimer's have all been linked to abnormalities of the glutamate system. Genes regulate the activity of a neurotransmitter in the brain are more abundant in depressed women than men.

Women are two to three times more likely to attempt suicide, but men are four times more likely to die by suicide. The risk of suicide is associated with changes in several neurotransmitter systems," Sobetso reads out swiftly.

"So, you want me to get depressed and kill myself, die right. I cannot die for any. I love my life. I have a dream. I have to travel a lot to unknown places. And I trust my dream not you, explains Rosenlu, with a sigh of relief, looking out of the window of the Mishmi traditional house."

....Inner Conflicts halt....

It's three in the evening, Rosenlu along with Mihinlu and Raju, son of the School watchman goes to the river Digaru to bathe.

It is this river that inspires Rosenlu to dream. This river that churns the mystery in her mind. She wanted to follow the course of this river and discover where it ends.
****

It is this mystery that begin her journey. It was this dream she dreamt w hen she was in her early teenage. She will start living again, all by her own. She is in Uzanbazar, in Guwahati. She has taken up a rented house. Bishu Prasad Kataki is a kind and considerate, good-humoured sixty years old man. She was good in her studies. She graduated from Girls' Handique College, with Major in Psychology. In the meantime, she got married to Nipon Goswami.

What she has learnt is to be like Prometheus, steal the fire from gods and help the hapless escape from cold, hunger, darkness. And also instil in her people the sense of arts and science and scientific thoughts. Prometheus influenced her, has brought the revolutionary fire rising in her. Now, she too has stolen the fire from gods and let the Prometheus in her bring into play the symbol of man's creative power and freedom and progress as an instrument to live on. And the mystical retrograde in her higher consciousness taking her deeper into the inward journey of greater wisdom and understanding. Irony is what snapped the relation is the minutest misunderstands causing jealousness at odds in the relation. This parts of the problems sums up being part of life couldn't guarantee a harmony. The theories and tactics fail when conscious thoughts are truncated. And they parted sweetly from their bitter days without any complications.

Hardly, anyone knows they were married. But the marriage did not last. What lasted is this continuous flow of river Brahmaputra, where river Lauhatya merges never drying. Water might have left the banks. But the banks are still there, through battered by erosion.

****

She returned to her village in Danglat after a decade, nothing has changed the village, the river, trees except the town with few RCC buildings. The river flows enchantingly still nourishing the people and the village and treated equally to the forest and animals. Reassuring her rootedness as well, for herself, for her family, for her society that foisted her surreptitiously to embrace life. As if it's the first day of her life that the flashes from inside and insights, let her feel that she has just discovered a sense of freedom. But everything was like unwarranted cure-alls.

She goes to the school, the next day; it was quite a different feeling standing in the vast field of the school. Then as a child, as a teenager and now as a thirty years old lady. In between she has grown up as a brilliant human cognizing better, evolving from utopian to social to making of the scientific minds. All that parts of problems helped her discovering, in the process of reassessing the powerful methods of life-changing follow-up, all in the silence of the flowing river Lauhatya. She freed her inner spaces, freeing the feelings from guilt. But guilt for what? Why should guilt hunt, if you are not a criminal, a sinner. These spontaneous forward movements made her master in her teachings in more practical ways, soon after she joined the government Higher Secondary school as a social science teacher.
****

Rosenlu remarried her childhood friend, who was a widower, Sobetso. In the meantime, he had almost turned alcoholic. Drinking is a part of the ritual in the community and village. But not the way, the rituals dictate. Possessed by bad habit. The festival 'Tamlandu' and ritual like 'Bro' is observed for the well-being of health. But Sobetso's health was deteriorating. For the Mishimis, the deity Bro is Lord Shiva, where the sacred drinks, called Jholsei locally, are offered to deities by the

Priest call Kutwat. Drinks are indispensable. Alcoholism is rare, though.

It was shocking for Rosenlu to find Sobetso craving continuously without a break for a drink as soon as he is out of inebriated condition. The need for the drink, for him was running parallel to the need of oxygen to breathe. They dubbed their drink as "Liquid Oxygen" hard for people to decipher. The easy accessibility and mushrooming liquor shops licensed to sell unlimited IMFL, Indian Made Foreign Liquor was adding misery to the misfit. It further shocked her, as when she met him after a decade and for the first time as grown up. His behaviour charmed her. He was a charmer. But the truth is a totally surreal, so bizarre, and so unreal now. Dwell on this dichotomy of a mutual division of fallacies.

He would attempt to kill her if she delays giving money, her salary. He would take the cleaver and would chase out anyone in sight from the house. He starts treating everyone like an enemy. One day he fell on the blade of the plough, from the platform of the house. His injured his head. The blood gushed out. But he lay there painless, unconscious, unknown of the blood.

He was taken to the civil hospital, Tezu. He recuperated from unconsciousness, he looked around for Rosenlu. He could not move out, and then he saw his hands were cuffed. And the rope was tied in the handle of the bed.

"Rosenlu…. Rosenlu…," he started shouting.

Police appeared that calmed him.

He looked at the handcuff. Then looked up at the police, appallingly.

"Leave me. Remove all this, he shouted at the cops and jerked the hands."

He hit his hands against the bed. Then the nurses came running. Tying his fingers and legs with the strings made of bandages.

He was calmed down by the doctors.

Sobetso enquired about Rosenlu.

"Ït's not yet confirmed, she is dead or not. But we discovered a blood-stained cleaver. And your body lying on the pool of blood," said the police, non-leniently.

"But the blood on the cleaver doesn't match your blood. And your wife is missing. Village people have complained that she had been murdered," continued the police.

Rosenlu didn't dare to share the worst ever ordeals to anyone. She thought Sobetso will come out clean. But for another five years taking care of Sobetso has pushed her into the brink of bankruptcy and now hereness, helpless. She left teaching. Her hopelessness led to transact with hard fate. Her dream to bring prosperity and well-being to her village and society crumble like a castle of sands.

Now, nobody knows where Rosenlu vanished. What was found as evidence, was the blood-stained cleaver, in that night that led people to presume that Rosenlu is dead. They searched her in the river Digaru too. Where she would often go and sit by its bank for long hours. For the people of Danglat, Rosenlu is dead.

****

"How could you allege sexual abuse resulting from sexual attack? "Yes, I agree usually it's out of an envious act."

"Now, tell Jantee. Did you rape her? Feel free I am a friend first then an advocate convinces Jahnavi Borthakur.

"Darn, I tried to help her out. I saw her in Bus station. I gave her my shirt to wear. Her clothes were all torn. She was almost in a bare body, explains Jantee Borbora."

"I didn't rape her, how can helping be raping," murmurs Jantee to himself.

"As because there is no relevant evidence. People, how easily can think of sexual exploits. Do you think women are capable of that....

"Sex! No that was consensual, I mean had to be consensual. Even if both never liked each other."

Attraction! Sudden attraction is the perpetrator.

I knew Rosenlu as Nipon Goswami's wife. And I didn't know the marriage didn't last. Few years of togetherness, then there was minor frays, we were aware of. But they were a long match.

Yes, that human behaviour to be with each other, to be there, stick to the relation.

What kind of attraction!

Use affectionate language! Continued Jantee trying to explain, trying to get a clear picture of what happened the night he saw Rosenlu.

"Is she on facebook? "enquired Jahnavi.

"No, she is known for her extreme dislike to socialize," replied Jantee.

How do you know?

Jahnavi, I need to clean up the mess. If you stop interrogating me.

Tell me about the blood.

"No, it's from her menstruation, she was menstruating then," replied Jantee cleaning up the dining table.

"She was taken to the behavioural hospital. But she was okay....Then to Correctional home. In the mental institution," continued Jantee.

"Restitution cost?" asked Jahnavi.

"Who will pay? Are you mad? She was okay....sticky situation is she was pregnant. She ran out of the house nude in the middle of the night and spent the night on the pedestal," said Jantee.

" Then, then and there, yes, at last she was freed to go....she was clean. We were wrong about her in the whole time.It was the man she loved was an addict. Drunk as a skunk. Obviously once drunk they would see a pink elephant. The visual hallucination arising from heavy drinking, they can kill any at that particular time," explains Jantee while cleaning up the mess in the bathroom, brushing the stains of blood.

"Skunk drinks, they know about alcohol or drugs," gags Jahnavi.

"Aren't you yourself an addict," asked Jahnavi.

"Yes, I was eight years old, when I, out of curiosity, tasted the first drop of Alcohol," I had to confess, as a forty years old Alcoholic Anonymous."Slowly in thirty years I became an addict. I started walking nude, sleep on pavements, anywhere in the city corners on roads, for six to seven hours, I was saved many times from running over by vehicles. Rather being too selfish, further gripped by a false sense of power, a false sense of achievement. Started perceiving, after consuming that I am superior to any normal human being, with supreme power equal to God, I had to continue to confess as a Recovering AA.

"I used to see everyone as a threat. This led me to almost kill one of my friends. I once strangled my wife almost to death. Many such fatal incidents happened beyond my conscious. I started abusing anyone, scare them away. Slowly, people stopped visiting me. All this mindless acts, under the inebriated condition, confessing honestly ruined the prime time of my life, I failed to taste the essence of hard work, challenges, competition. I could not succeed to be compassionate, to be a giver, to be a lover overall, I lost all in my values, in the transition from human being to becoming a beast. I failed to acknowledge that my family cares me and love me a lot," he would talk ceaselessly as Jahnavi listens to him patiently.

"But I didn't kill her," he would confess but lost in thought.

"SUFFERERS ARE THE CARE-GIVERS, I realized that."

Rosenlu would call me up and tell how she is taking care of Sobelso. And all that is dark. But she didn't know, I also had caused the same suffering to my wife.

"Yes, my wife (whom I married, without letting her know that I am an alcoholic, I was not honest. I killed my honesty first then her, I ruined her life, ruined her peace of mind, she is under severe depression. When she saw me walking out of the house drunk and walk nude. She being teetotaller- anti-alcohol. It was shocking for her. Something new, unknown, hallucinatory.

The craving was such, I would walk out anytime midnight to dawn to any odd hours. I had money that I don't allow anyone to touch, I knew only my wallet. Funny that the only thing I was possessive about my wallet and the money in it. I know the places and person the drug peddlers, vendors- the small shops, every nook and corner, even too inaccessible areas, who sells all these drugs and drinks twenty-four hours. So, finding this substance was easy.

Once I am out of my inebriated state. I tend to create disturbances if I don't get a bottle. The restlessness and craving are fatal, I will go mad. My innocent family, out of fear and anger or to retain momentary peace would help me cater drink. But that was a non-stop, 24 hours of craving.

They would yell at me with a warning,"The last stage of an alcoholic, this could cause cirrhosis, stroke, heart attack, failure of any organ that leads to death."

They were still ignorant about these strokes and tremors caused to me. They are used to this nuisance and disturbances that for them it's normal. They didn't know it is a medical complication. But apart from medical treatment. The basic treatment I needed was a holistic approach to overall by being- the psychological, mental, physical, social and most importantly spiritual. A mere medical intervention will not and never help.

The actual disease is in the mind. They do not have hopes, will, courage, love. This creates a vacuum. They live on the vacuum. Which I personally felt the killer vacuum inside. And to fill it up and to escape from all this foolishness and timidity, one end up in the slow process of poisoning. Everything inside fell apart.

My confused family was baffling with ignorance. My friends would laugh at me and say, "Gone case". It's because of my friends influence I started this deadly journey, they too could have helped me, they are rich but spoilt and selfish too, today they see me lying on the footpath, and when I was hungry- I ate the food from the drain of the hotel.

They laughed at me. My family was in shame. But, we are not that in a state to think that we are shaming the family's dignity and wipe out the integrity.

I was dying. But for me that was a normal life. The feelings and acceptance to this have sunk so deep inside. Truly, for us that's normal.

But after leaving alcohol for a decade, I could feel this pure bliss. I avoid all the friends. I won't blame them, though there are alcohol users also in my family-they too, to some extend influence me, which aggravated the situation to worsen. Without alcohol no celebration of birthdays, success, even failure, even to mourn death. Today, I find this most degenerating, when my mother died, whom throughout her life I have hurt, my friends know that I am an alcoholic, they got me a bottle to find solace in my mourning. But they didn't know, I deride this act. I threw the bottle away and said sorry to the departed soul of my mother. It relieved me from the reparation.

I was an Alcohol abuser. I would go to parties' family or friends, weddings and birthdays in sobriety but would in the meantime take a chance, binge drink beyond control and would end up messing and creating a scene, spoil the auspicious moments without a sense of guilt. And many unpleasant things went on, for many years in my prime time. Slowly, everyone started avoiding me.

My family loves me most, its proved now, but I abused them a lot, even I used to treat as my slave. Today, I am fortunate, so blessed that today I am a confident man, my wife loves me besides the fact that I was an alcoholic and I was dying a slow death. She is considerate enough, emphatic.

In the process of treatment and counselling. My family including my wife came to know that Alcoholism is also a disease. A deadly disease which has no cure. It proved that it's a vicious circle - a death trap, once one gets trapped, escaping from responsibilities and sensibilities was easy, and now escaping from this death-trap is not possible. It's like a quagmire, you slowly sink into the dark, and finally life leaves you.

Today, I as a recovering addict, but also I feel free from sinning, free from guilt, lying. I live an honest and happy life now. I sleep in peace. I know how peaceful and healing sleep is, truly I can relate to the beauty of fairy tale-" sleeping beauty". It's been almost ten years I do not take drugs in any form alcohol, or other pharmaceutical chemicals to ganja to opium to painkillers to cough syrups, LSD, phencyclidine the-angel dust. All the powerful effects of hallucinogenic ecstasy ....and escape.

It's really the biggest blunder and foolishness to be a chemical dependent. The journey from Curiosity as a grown up child of eight to almost alcohol user teenage to abuser adult. I was literally in the mouth of death. Yes, now my preamble is always stick to the winners-the winning attitude in you(material gain is not winning,

winning my helping and becoming a giver) "ABC" Always, Avoid Bad Company" as because you are responsible and conscious individual, who has just taken a new birth-aptly resurrection - a chance to live an honest and beautiful second life. I have been taught and inculcated in me a value of life, relation and duty. So, I cannot avoid duty. My duty today is to help those in millions, who is living a life of hell that I led. It's a deadly disease which needs holistic approach-total care. "

My FAMILY WAS IN SHAME AND IN DOOM, I had to Confess:

"Everybody would avoid me, won't even care to take my name. Even my family were confined to the dark world, they feel ashamed to face the society. They too started avoiding, going places out of shame. Because, I am their only son, who have caused all these shame, sufferings and pain to them."

"Yes, the Alcoholic doesn't die alone-they takes along them the whole family to doom, towards disaster and finally towards death. Because each member, each individual in the family suffers along, because of the addict, that leads slowly to depression. And depression is also such a deadly disease that leads to death. Today, I make an attempt and try my best to help all the addicts to cure them of this deadly disease. Most importantly, we act as a healer-healing agent to the family who too suffers whose integrity and spirit is totally shattered." The recovering addict is happy in a decade-long service has brought the pride of family back.

The addiction cost lots of money. I sold off my ancestral home at Rs. 15 lakhs and it took few months to blow that money off into alcohol and treating friends with alcohol. The only source of enjoyment is drugs, in the form of alcohol. We become slaves to drugs. Few of my friends have to end up being criminals too. They lost their sense, lost their control and in an inebriated condition, molestation, to abuses to murdering people. They fail to recognize anyone. They may exercise unprotected sex with multiple partners, which could lead to unwanted pregnancy, sexually transmitted disease and HIV/AIDS.

I CAME OUT CLEAN: BUT AS AN ADDICTS-RECOVERING I NEEDED EXTRA CARE.

My health deteriorated, the wounds from the continues push, the flesh was rotting, stinking. But my wife took it as a challenge. And she could.

At the same time, Rosenlu's telephonic talks made me realize fast. Where I was heading. The ordeal she went through while taking care of her alcoholic husband. Also saving herself from the fatal acts of attempts to kill her. The killer instinct influenced by the alcohol, that impairs his reasoning and feelings, he turns to killer then, suddenly when he is out of inebriated state. It's hard to see them sobers down and acts like God. Behaviour becomes very unpredictable. You lose trust bit by bit. The more you want to trust, to save the relation, the more you drift apart.

As an AA, I continue to confess. "Today, I am clean. I am dedicating my service to help out and save a precious life. I have gained my respect back. Before my family and friends use to avoid me feel ashamed to take my name. Today when they see me on television sharing the truth, trying my best to help other addicts-who are in their first, specifically the kids. And the dying in their Final stage, saving them from dying, is my reward. They understand the causes and effects of addiction rather this deadly disease. It's difficult. But they feel proud of me. And this made me more responsible.

But today I have realized it has petrifying dimension because of an uncontrollable situation. There are loopholes, that are hard to detect. But the only solution is a total ban of this drug. Again there will be a failure to check illegal selling by bootleggers. Authorities turn deaf and blind towards illegal selling. I don't know, is it a matter of pride when excise department earns in corers in a year. Prohibitions and bans but again that are lifted. As even it is believed by policymakers that prohibition increases the use and other related crimes. That's the tragedy of prohibition.

That's what I feel. The disease is in the minds of the people. That is to be cured. Once people realize the true love to live life. Nobody can force them to drink.

"That's my life, Jahnavi," sighs Jantee.

You, women, are healers too; you not only give births to life.

Whatever you three are doing for the society, one day the world shall recognize your efforts.

Jahnavi was in a total trance as if she was lost watching a cinema. The knock in the door brought Jahnavi out of her transcendental mind.

Gargee brings in four cups of ginger-tea, everybody's favourite. Especially, when its made by Gargee.

"So, this tea has kept the husband-wife love alive, right," Jahnavi taunts at Jantee and Gargee.

"Four Cups! And we are three," exclaims Jantee.

"Our Rosenlu is here, she will be honoured for her contribution in eradicating alcoholism and her dedication in making her dream come true, she is on the way," announces Gargee.

Award! Rosenlu! Our Prometheus- the God's fire-stealer. What are all these surprises....exclaimed Jantee?

Jantee looked back when he saw Gargee and Jahnavi smiling towards the door.

Rosenlu appears wearing her Daflaithanga, Mishmi traditional dress. And Gamusa- the traditional Assamese stole on her shoulder. The Japi-Assamese traditional hat in her hand. Bouquet of flowers, memtos.

"Tea then talk," demands Rosenlu.

Congratulations Rosenlu! You made us feel proud.

Thank you for this life! Thank you Jantee for all your quotes including that Homers quote-The man does better who runs from a disaster then he who is caught by it, and I really had to run away from all the quagmires, it was total enervation. Not the unconventional enfant terrible but the killer instincts. Enfilade fire! So, different like chalk and cheese from Prometheus stolen God's fire. With this fire in me now, I don't know how better I can work for the children, save them, save the future, what would be the final denouement from all these convolutions," puts forth Rosenlu.

"Danglat is still waiting for you," reminds Jantee.

" Humanity can be served from any corner of the world though the earth is flat," replies Rosenlu.

Frugal about every minutes, time is life now. Tragedies of life can be compared to Great depression, which will eternally remind anyone to be sparing. So stitch life to shape up. Life cannot be in godlessness. It's a beatific bliss. But Jantee, it like shards to believe a person who is dwell on trivialities, suddenly shift to such earth-shattering matters. Suddenly, so unplayful, that's dull of a saintly inexperienced sinner, enfant sauvage," jokes Rosenlu.

"Intellectual sympathy for the depressed soul, huh, so sporadic sometimes, mercurial, whimsical, volatile. unstable, infirm, these are like the pseudorandom number generator are important to generate and practice reproducibility, Yes, I like being saintly sinner-the enfant sauvage cannot be dubbed as enfant terrible," said Jantee then laughs out loud.

A burst of laughter merged along the steams from the cups of hot tea, forming patterns then vanished in the air. All of them went to watch a movie. There was a rush for the ticket. Few ticket left in the front row. Jantee had to buy it. The poster was not that interesting, but Kangana Ranaut acted quiet good, revolutionary. The impact of cinema not bad. Rosenlu felt bit good watching Queen, liberated and restored.

Next morning Rosenlu prepares a note to address in her next seminar...

Don't limit a child to your own learning. For he was born in another time. By Rabindranath Tagore. Starting with this line because my focus is on children.

Because in my research related to this I was with many AA or NA confesses honestly, the early use of drugs.

There are stubborn hurdles in finding the effective solutions to deal with this disease. A serious progressive illness as lakhs of addicts are succumbed to the impulsive and compulsive craving for mood altering substances. Families too become a victim and suffer from shame and isolation. It shatters the dreams, expectations and hopes of families to see their children as a successful person. Once this slow process of disease show up a disaster, helpless hide the illness in their homes, degrading the self-respect, morals and values of each member, which are essential for a healthy growth of family and life.

FREEDOMS are not only the primary ends of development, they are also among its principal…. Amartya Sen's concept of development as freedom. His concept of human development is about the expansion of citizens capabilities. Who will be this citizen? Who will be part of this development if in the stage of growth and development they are invisibly deviating towards disaster? Children trapped in this disaster cannot see a better tomorrow.

Gujarat is the only state is the only state with a death penalty for makers and sellers of homemade liquors, the rapid action was taken because the deaths caused by consumption. If a person is literally poisoned to death is a crime termed as murder. Alcohol selling and offering is also a crime, slow poisoning a murder.

True, the honest confession was benumbing but was broadly an eye-opener. The wrong taste of curiosity, the wrong experiment ruined a person life. Though, addiction is not curable. They live in the process of recovery. AA also affirms that we are recovered totally from addiction- this deadly disease after death.

I avoid going out or social visits. I avoid my friends for fear of RELAPSE AND WITHDRAWAL SYMPTOMS. Anyday, AA/NA can relapse. AA for Alcoholic Anonymous. NA stands for Narcotics Anonymous.

If they start meeting people who use these drugs call alcohol, chemicals. Anyday, they can relapse, they need to follow up the steps to recovery. Yes, on a certain condition, with sheer determination of power and will of the user of drugs to give up, might help. But mere will might fail. Once they start meeting friends, moods and environment. They might relapse. They should inculcate in them the power to say "NO" boldly and with confidence. Then the recovering addict might continue to live a healthy life again.

Both AA and NA can still live a sober life. If they are spiritually, mentally and physically strong. Spiritual enlightenment, surrender to divine higher power supports them in optimum to be an optimist.

CRAVINGS are Allergy.

"I can control. I know when to stop", the user may feel. Infact, they cannot, they are powerless, and the addicts are weak, when it comes to craving. They lose their senses. They can resort to criminal activities. The process of addiction has no full stop. Once used, it starts affecting the body and brain. The user craves further intake, increasing the probability of addiction.

QUITTING BUT MEDICAL INTERVENTION MUST

As withdrawal symptoms might cause heart stroke or organ failure or could lead to death. Medical treatment is highly recommended. A drug user must be taken to a detoxification and rehabilitation centre. Proper medical, family and emotional support help the recovering addict.

IF YOU CANNOT HELP: DON'T STIGMATIZE

An addict needs help. Help them to feel loved. Gift them those hopes, dream, will, confidence and support to revive. When regains will-power and confidence, starts a new life. This is their second birth. A chance to start all over again. The responsibility of each individual to have empathy-the power to understand. After lots of suffering and pain, the drug addict's attempts to come out clean. They need help. Don't stigmatize a drug user.

Being a good human, it's our responsibility to help. If a drug user is in its initial stage. Friends, family and elders can help to make him understand of the hazard.

If the abuse habit is more advanced. Professional counselling and de-addiction centre can be of help.

Never be against them.

PSYCHOLOGICAL HEALTH

Check the psychological growth of children. If you care for their future.

SPIRITUAL HEALTH

If the foundation is strong building automatically will be strong. School can help in the development of a well-balanced personality in a child through the various programme, which will help in the healthy growth of physical, Mental and Spiritual abilities of a child. Learn and teach them too, to control anger and greed. Teach them to be a giver.

Sometimes, strict disciplinary measures taken in school causes mental disorder in the students at the same time, uncontrolled freedom my encourage them to involve in anti-social activities. A way to attain self-discipline is of higher priority. Counsellors' play a vital role in maintaining a proper mental health. They must be taught to express anger, fear, respect, sadness in a socially desirable manner.

A preservation of proper mental attitude must be provided to develop proper sentiments, feelings, healthy attitude towards life. Misconceptions on Sex education.

MENTAL EDUCATION

Society has high moral expectations from teachers.

A child spends a maximum of its time in the school. As this is the place of learning, focusing on the development of friendly and positive attitude can prevent the mental illness by improving mental health. So, to inculcate all these values that will be the causes of their successful healthy life. For this Mental, health and attitudes of the teachers should be of high integrity, with their sense and essence of their responsibility in making rather deciding the fate of their future. Otherwise, it would be that hard if the easily gravitate towards the lurking powerful death trap.

They can anyday at any age i.e. seven-eight years old onwards, lean on addiction. Start with the drop out of curiosity and develop thrill in the process.

COVER UP: FAMILY, SOCIAL AND CULTURAL ACCEPTANCE

Alcohol is both socially and culturally acceptable. The user may say they aren't just alcoholic or abuser. It's really not true, it slowly encourages powerlessness.

Any person in the name of ritual or religion or custom or celebration is another advantage they take. Instead, it is clinically suggestive to be aware of its slow process towards damaging effect to death. In a way, the user can take advantage of the different aspect and representation of the particular drug that causes hazard each day crippling the user and the world he is surrounded with. Once they are addicted. Parents try to cover up their child's bad habit. Most important step is to help themselves, in finding a way in the understanding of the consequences and some of the reasons users of drugs struggle with cravings. And look ahead the importance of healthy life and find resources to transform such situation with proper activities and event.

URGENCY TO TACKLE

It is now an urgent need to keep a constant watch on the behaviour of users. It's not a question of responsible or irresponsible users, which ultimately had led to the disruption of peaceful co-existence. Families are ruined.

Emphasis is given more on the care and support of affected person. Not only medical treatment can help recover the person but overall the holistic approach is mandatory. They together need to act on a war-footing to ensure   enforcing proper vigil, dissemination of knowledge about its crippling effect of slow death.

DISEASE OF THE MIND.

There is a myth and misconception in the minds of the people that Alcoholism or substance abuse is a bad habit. But the bitter truth is it's a deadly disease, disease of the mind. The death toll across in North-East India alone crosses thousands in a year. Overall, in India almost lakhs die in a year.

Chemical dependency (CD) in India has grown at an alarming rate. And in North East CD has spread at an unprecedented growth rate despite growing awareness.

DREAMS TURNS NIGHTMARES

Everyone dreams to become someone great and plans for future. And start living a dream.

But in the process to reach the dream. One simple mistake takes away the life.

"TRY ONCE" is what most friends - adolescents, teenage ask to. They dwell on the myth that taking drugs is the indicator of their being rich or have higher social-economic status, higher confidence, and independence. These are the superiority complex they suffer from, as a consequence. Avoid friends, who insist you to test or try substance.

Living on a myth, that addiction is a symbol of pride and richness. This disease finally cripples anyone regardless of age, sex, caste, religion.

Slowly, they fail to cope with everyday life. As a result, they escape.

CELEBRITIES: FAMOUS PERSONALITIES

Influences from addicted celebrities, legends are fast and powerful.

The users start following certain notion, rather a false sense of achievements. They start imitating the most of the celebrities both legends and new-avatars who themselves are abusers and addicts.

ESCAPISM: RESPONSIBILITIES AND BOREDOM

Devils truly dwell in empty minds. The absence of social and recreational activities.

Peer pressure is the main cause of depression. Weak people fall prey easily to drugs to escape rejection, isolation, blackmails, or to cover up weaknesses. And altogether the Stress, emotional insecurity, family problems, lack of self-discipline and self-respect and self-control. They fail to cope up with life and attempts to escape from all these problems. They attempt to escape from all these problems. And start depending totally on drugs.

REFUSALS KILLS: POWERFUL "NO" TO DRUGS
There is hundred and one way to enjoy life or escape boredom rather than drugs. Refusing is a powerful skill. Starting here means no stopping. Those who do drugs for fun, to enjoy, fails to realize that in true sense this choice or this form of enjoyment makes enjoyment in the true sense a distant dream. If one has the power to say NO, it is a bold statement for those who love life, who value living. Life surely is a pure bliss for them.

EASY AVAILABILITY OF DRUGS
Sedatives, stimulants and party drugs like ecstasy. The victim varies from teenage to officers to professional to businessmen. Female addicts are growing, in shockingly alarming rate.

Another greatest threat is the volatile inhalants such as dendrite and erazex, which are being abused and inhaled by children as young as 7years. So far, more than 4000 street children in a city like Guwahati are glue sniffing addicts. The city becomes the breeding ground for these children, who in the course of time become criminals. There are more wine shops than schools.

PREVENTION IS THE WEAPON: ROLE OF PARENTS, TEACHER, COMMUNITIES

Addiction is a process. Prevention is the sole double edge sword, the weapon, the remedy to cure and cut the growing graphs of this disease. Teachers, parents and society together with holistic approach can tackle these dangerous situations before it's too late. They should be warned of medical complications. The growing wine shops are adding fuel to the fire. The concerned government departments and specialized NGOs cannot tackle these growing epidemics. Overall, the community participation, women organization, youth clubs, educational institutions, teachers, medical practitioners, a religious based organisation at par need to check the growing epidemic and enormity of challenge it requires. A collective effort to face the threat is required to stop this rapid transitory phase of our society.

A multi-dimensional level with primary concern to accept addiction as a major threat to life. Social, family and individual denial have to be removed to end this epidemic.

STRONG PEOPLE HAVE THE WILL-POWER TO SAY NO TO DRUGS. SAYING "NO TO DRUGS" IS A BOLD STATEMENT.

It was 1.a.m. in the morning, she didn't have patient left to recheck what points she jotted down for next day's Awareness programme. Away from the eye of issues, her beautiful eyes, like the watchfully painted eyes on Egyptian frescoes, called for a sleep. A good sleep was what all she needed.

Heena Ahuja

Heena Ahuja, a Mumbai girl at heart is an avid reader. Reading fiction caught her fancy when she stumbled across Sidney Sheldon, J.D Robb, Dan Brown & Nicholas Sparks books. After completing her masters she found her true calling in writing and has a lot of English poems published under her belt in various e-magazines and columns and few Hindi poems have been published in a Delhi based newspaper. She loves listening to music and learning new things about life. She really wishes to travel and explore places and capture memories in her camera. She is a poetess at heart and ends up pouring her heart on a paper. She along with her co-author Meghant Parmar has marked her debut in the world of writing with a short story in "Uff Ye Emotions-2". Her solo short story titled "Slaves of Soul" was part of "Fusion-A Mingled Flavour Mocktail" which came out from Dream

House Publisher's stable. She has a full time Facebook page where people have admired and adored her writing too. You can connect with her through her Facebook writing page and blog too.

http://literatimeraki.blogspot.in/

Reverberating Soulful Silence

Let's, on this take a chance
Match the steps of a groovy dance,
As silent storm reverberates my soul
Pealing off the dirt and desires foul.
Breaking my woebegone state
It drowns me in their dreamy skate,
Released from my dark abyss
It guides me into a trance of bliss.
Chirp melodies of hilarity they say
Keeping my heart all happy and gay.
Silent screams that terrified me once
Now they don't have my energy's ounce,
My heart is free from fears, horrendous
As life smiles back at me, stupendous.

<u>Anuja Bhatia</u>

She is a fun loving girl who hails from Faridabad and enjoys the company of her friends. She likes to write poems and most of her poems are spontaneous. A few of her poems have been published already. She agrees with Wordsworth's view that
"Good poetry is a spontaneous overflow of emotions."
Her poetry depicts her emotions. She likes to write about nature and society. She s a spiritual being and believes in God and his powers. She also believes in Karma and destiny. And so she tries not to hurt others either intentionally or unintentionally.

Over Thinking

Over fed by thoughts, the mind keeps thinking,
The gaze is fixed but the eyes keep blinking.
Forming innumerable concentric circles of assumptions,
The brain doesn't succumb to get peace and
concentration.
The mind battles the assumptions to get free,
but thoughts metamorphose from a plant to form a tree.
This tree then bears the sour fruits of depression,
Many a times, because there's a lack of expression.
Once a happy soul, the soul now feels shattered,
Also, the hopes and dreams and joys look scattered.
But the roots of such trees should be soon cut down
So that there's positivity all around, and mind paves way
to the new happy town.

Would 'IT' Remain A Taboo

Too many mouths that shouted out loud,
why was it that her identity was covered in a shroud?
She was just a girl of twenty
According to the society, the probability of her indulging
Into 'the act' was the least, and not plenty.

With her boyfriend had she rejoiced
But her dignity and image in the society was time and
again voiced
She didn't know that a soft kiss
Would take away her life's bliss

She didn't understand why an 'act of pleasure'
was disregarded and questioned?
Was she the only one who got into 'the act'?
This haunted her mind and left her stunned.

'You have disgraced us' shouted her father.
'Don't worry. It's okay' she would have loved to listen
rather!
No one wanted to talk about 'that'
Why in the society is 'it' unacceptable and bad?

Till when would 'it' be a taboo?
Would sex, the pleasurable act,
the most natural instinct be always referred to as 'that'?

The Violent World

There was this child of seven,
Unaware of the happenings on earth and in heaven.
Poor lad couldn't comprehend what was going on,
Because there was no one to explain and he was all alone.
Hiding under the table, he looked for his mother
Except for a few corpses around, he couldn't find
anything other.
Trembling and terrified, he went near a cadaver
Finding it to be his mother's, he cried,
then wiped his tears, and thought why did someone kill
her ?
So many questions popped up in his mind,
and there was no answer that he could find.
His heart was all broken and cold,
so he let his tears roll down, because no more he could
hold.

Divya Bandodkar

Divya R. Bandodkar hails from Ponda, a town in the state of Goa. She has contributed stories in 12 anthologies so far. Minds @ Work 4 is her 13th anthology and first publication with First Step Publishing. Reading and writing are her favorite hobbies. She has recently discovered her knack in book reviewing and has been associated with two review firms. You can know more about her by visiting her blog.

http://musingsofavivaciousheart.blogspot.in/

Everything has been planned

I sat on the bed, buttoning my shirt. He lay back on the bed, watching me getting dressed.

"You have a very sexy back," He said while ruffling his fingers through his hair.

"Kabir, you haven't answered my question yet. I am waiting for your answer." I replied curtly.

"Come on Payal. I am in a good mood today. Please don't spoil it."

"I am not planning to spoil your mood, Kabir. I just need an answer. Is the question so difficult?" I turned around to look at him.

"Payal."

"Kabir, I am your fiancée. Can't you answer me?" He pulled me towards him. His hands got busy in unbuttoning my shirt. He buried his mouth in the nape of my neck and started kissing me.

"Stop it, Kabir! I need to go to see my patients."

"Shhh! Just 2 more minutes."

"Kabir, I will be back soon," I said as I placed a kiss on his lips.

"I will miss you," He said, making a puppy face.

"Kabir, keep your answer ready!" I smiled as I walked out through the door.

It's been almost a week that I am questioning Kabir. Every time, he avoids answering it. I was determined to make him answer me today. But could not do so! We had made ourselves time today, almost after 3 months. This too was forced upon by Kabir.

Being doctors, we had never found time for ourselves. Surgeries and patients always kept us busy. Kabir is a gynaecologist and I am an intern. Dating for 5 years had ultimately bore fruit and we got engaged six months ago. Kabir is senior to me by 4 years.

I reached my ward and made myself busy with my patients. Spending time with patients always brightened my day. They shared with me their life stories. Their stories were inspiring ones. I always believed that no matter how short one's story is, it always gives out a message to the listeners. You just need a knack of grasping that message.

"Rekha, how is Kanchan doing now?" I asked a lady whom I met at the entrance of the female general ward.

"She is devasted, Doctor Madam. She cannot bring herself to the fact that her baby is no more." Rekha explained.

I could do nothing but stare at Rekha. I was baffled by the courage she showed that day when she announced the death of Kanchan's baby to me. There weren't any tears in her eyes. She was acting strong for the sake of her sister. I envied her.

"Rekha, it is going to take time. She has lost her baby for the third time. I shall see you soon. I need to see my patients." I said and took her leave. I was, once again, brought back to the original question.

I rushed towards Kabir's room after finishing my round. I needed an answer today. I knocked on the door. Kabir did not answer. I took out the spare key from my purse and got myself inside. Kabir was sleeping peacefully, without the slightest frown on his face. He led a difficult life since the death of his parents. He says that he found new happiness after getting engaged to me. I too believe that he has faced many hardships. I feel sorry for him. My question was going to put him to test. I wanted him to be successful at it.

I changed into my nightwear and climbed onto the bed. Kabir sensed my presence and put his arm around me.

"Are you back, Sweety?" He asked.

"Yeah!" I answered in a low tone.

"Payal, your question has been haunting me like a ghost since past few days."

"Kabir, it's okay. We can talk tomorrow!" I kissed him.

"No Payal. It's not okay! I am afraid."

"Kabir, are you trying to say that you are involved?"

"Yes."

I remained immobile for a moment. Kabir's answer had shocked me.

"Kabir, Please say that you are lying to me. Please!"

"No Payal. I am not! I cannot lie to you anymore!"

"How long have you been doing this?"

"3 years." He hung his head in shame.

"I cannot believe this!"

"Please don't hate me, Payal. Please don't!"

"Kabir, I need some time to get through this!"

I turned to the side away from Kabir. Both of us silently wept. The reason was the same- breaking of trust. I recalled the day when all of this mess started.

***

"Doctor Madam! Doctor Madam! Please look at my sister. She is getting these pains continuously from past

24 hours." A lady clad in a clean but weary saree spoke to me.

"Where is your sister?" I asked her. She pointed to a lady in her late twenties with a big baby bump.

"She is 8 months pregnant." She declared.

"Okay! Let me check her!" I realised her bad health status and fetched my phone to call up Kabir.

"Kabir, where are you?"

"OPD No. 4" He answered.

"Come to the casualty immediately. It's an emergency." I hung up.

"How are you feeling now?" I asked the pregnant lady. She just nodded her head.

"What is your name?"

"Kanchan." She answered.

Kabir saw me sitting in the waiting area with Kanchan and her sister, Rekha. I gestured him to come near us. I explained everything about Kanchan to him.

"Kanchan, this is Kabir. He will look after you. Don't worry. You and your baby will be fine." I comforted her and left.

Later that night, Kabir and me, we went home (my place) for dinner. We never actually discussed our personal lives. Our talks, most of the times were related to surgeries, syringes and medicines.

"How is Kanchan doing?" I asked him. My mother threw a cruel frown at me.

"Maa, he is okay with it!" I said.

"Pretty fine! We are required to deliver her baby. Complications may arise later on. Hence, it is mandatory."

"C-section?"

"Let's see! I cannot say anything as of now. It depends on Deshpandey Sir."

"Payal, eat your food now. You can discuss your cases with him later on." My mother said.

"Yeah! He is all mine!" I pulled Kabir's cheeks.

(The next day)
I went to the Female General Ward to check my patients. I saw Kanchan sitting on the cot, smiling at me. I went to her to ask her about her health. She seemed very excited that her baby was coming soon. She was told that she would be shifted to the maternity ward soon. Lack of beds was stated as the reason for her being in the general ward. Government hospitals are unpredictable. You can never predict which patients will be allotted beds in which wards. I wished her luck and carried on with my work.

I did not meet Kanchan any time later. I had been allotted duty in the operation theatre. I bumped into Kabir a few times but couldn't talk to him. I was worried about Kanchan. This was the first time that I had felt an attachment for a patient- that too Kabir's patient. I do not know what attracted me towards her- her simplicity? Her smile? I really do not know. She had very expressive eyes. Though her happiness, her excitement was visible on her face, she was terrified. Her eyes conveyed it to me. I wanted to know the story behind that fear. I wished to be a part of that secret that her eyes were concealing from the world.

***

The sun had dawned clearing away all the darkness for the world but not for us. I was terribly upset with Kabir. He had let me down.

"Good morning, Payal. Didn't you sleep well last night?"

"I slept well." I answered without looking at him.

"Your puffed eyes and runny nose narrate some other story!"

I did not say anything. He turned me towards him and stared into my eyes.

"Why Kabir? Why did you do this?" I asked.

"I did not do it deliberately Payal. Everything had been planned by Deshpandey Sir. I feel sorry for acting like a puppet. Trust me Payal! I did not have any other option."

"What do you want to do?"

"Are you upset with me?"

"Yes, Kabir. I am!"

Kabir made a sad face. I knew that he was hurt for he had hurt me. I knew that he was not faking sadness.

"How much were you paid for keeping your mouth shut?"

"Rs. 10000 per case."

"And how much money did Deshpandey Sir make?"

"I do not know."

"How long have you been doing this?"

"About 3 years." He lowered his eyes. Yes, he was repenting about his choice. I felt a pinch of happiness within me for this gesture.

"Have you seen how devasted she is?" Kabir kept looking at the ground.

"She has suffered this for the third time, Kabir. How could you be such a stone hearted person?"

"Payal."

"Are you regretting your decision, Kabir?"

"Yes. I am!"

"Will you help me in giving justice to her?"

"Yes, Payal."

"Kabir, I have some pieces of evidence with me. All I need is your support. Everything has been planned."

"I will." Kabir said.

I smiled and kissed him.

"I am happy to have you back." He declared.

"I did not leave you alone anytime, Kabir. It's just that I wanted you to willingly get out of this mess!"

***

(A week ago)

I received the greatest shock of my life from Rekha, Kanchan's sister.

"Doctor Madam! Kanchan's baby died."

"What?"

"Yeah! Doctor Sir told that they tried saving her baby but weren't successful."

"Oh! I am so sorry!" Kanchan's case file grabbed my attention. I discovered a strong urge within me to go through it. I was stunned to see her reports. All were declared to be normal. I sensed something fishy.

"Was it a girl?" I asked them.

"Yes!" They said in unison.

"I am taking your file for some time. In case Kabir comes looking for it, tell him that it's with me."

The reports clearly state that Kanchan had delivered a boy. Why did Kabir tell them that baby was a girl? Is Kabir hiding something from me? I must ask him.

I dialled Kabir and told him to meet me in the canteen.

"Is everything alright? You seemed worried over the phone!"

"I am fine, Kabir. Has Kanchan's baby girl expired?"

"Oh Yes! We couldn't save her."

"Why do the reports state that she delivered a boy?"

"What nonsense are you speaking, Payal?"

"Am I blabbering nonsense? Kabir, you can fool your patients but not me. I understand medical terminologies very well."

"Are you accusing me Payal?"

"No. I am not. I am just trying to find out the truth."

"You won't find any truth because I haven't lied at all."

"Time will tell, Kabir."

I was angry. And so had Kabir lost his temper. I did not know whether Kabir was speaking the truth or lying. I wished that he spoke the truth.

I marched into the female general ward to do some research. Being an intern, I could visit any ward at any hour of the day. Kabir's fiancée added more weight to it. I made a mental note of Kabir's patients and checked their files. I clicked the pictures of the reports. I made sure that nobody had noticed me taking the pictures. The reports would lead me to the truth.

After two hours of continuous study, I had found out some truth. A step more and Kabir would have faced a checkmate. I had planned everything. I went to Mrs Parker and chatted with her. I introduced myself as Kabir's fiancée to her and slowly took out all the information that I needed. I had kept the voice recorder on. Every single word had been recorded. I had found powerful evidence.

The day came to an end and I found myself in Kabir's room.

"Aren't you going to answer me, Kabir?"

"What question are you talking about?"

"Kanchan."

"You have gone crazy, Payal. You need some rest." He said and tucked me into the bed.

"Kabir, please answer me!"

"Payal, it's a stupid question. Go to sleep."

Going to sleep did not satiate my thirst for knowing the truth. So what if Kabir hadn't supported me? I had my ways of getting the truth out of him. I did not mention about my meeting with Mrs Parker to Kabir. That night, I slept determined to find out more evidence.

A week of research and I had finally gathered enough evidence to prove that baby trafficking was going on in our hospital. A confession from Kabir would be of incredible benefit. I hadn't spoken to Kabir for the entire week. I stayed in the hospital for the nights.

Yesterday night, I found Kabir in the Doctor's room of the female general ward. I was very happy to see him. But I did not show it to him. I wanted him to feel that his presence in the room hadn't affected me at all.

"How long are you going to ignore me?" He asked.

"Kabir, I am working. We shall talk about this later." I said with a stern look on my face. He did not move an inch.

"Kabir, all interns have gone out because of your presence here. Please go away now. I shall talk to you tomorrow." I said and opened the door.

Kabir came forward and closed the door.

"Not so soon!" He said and pinned me onto the door. He lowered his mouth on mine and started kissing me. It was hard for me to resist the kiss. It had been a week that I hadn't talked to him, hugged him. I had missed him badly. I gave in and an hour later, we both were lying spent, in each other's arms on his bed.

***

(Present)

"What do you want me to do?" Kabir asked.

"Everything has been planned, Kabir. I shall record your confession. I have talked to the media. They will interview you as soon as I forward your voice clip to them. They are in the hospital premises at present."

"I am nervous." He admitted.

"So am I. But we can do this, Kabir. Nothing can break us now!"

"Our jobs are at stake, Payal."

"No Kabir. They aren't. We are casting some light on the truth."

"Okay."

"Are you ready?"

"Yes." I put on the voice recorder and Kabir started speaking.

"I am Kabir, a senior resident of ABC Hospitals. I need to confess something to all of you. Baby trafficking has been happening in our hospital since last three years. Babies of poor people are sold off for lakhs to the rich. Dr.

Deshpandey has been carrying out this operation. I too was lured into this. But my fiancée, Payal, helped me come out of it and share the truth with all of you. We have gathered enough pieces of evidence to prove our confession. We cannot share the name of the patient involved. But the baby boy of the patient was sold off to a rich whose baby girl had died at the time of delivery. I know that our jobs are at stake. I feel proud that I confessed the truth. I feel like a true doctor today."

"Good work, Kabir. I am proud of you." I said and sent the voice clip over WhatsApp to the media person.

"They will be coming for you, Kabir. You will be taken. I am happy you did this for me."

"I did this for us, Payal."

"I really love you, Kabir."

"I love you too." We shared a passionate kiss and Kabir left.

I observed him carefully as he walked to the door. I knew that time was running out but suppressed the urge to check my watch. I took a deep breath and started counting in reverse under my breath. "Ten, nine, eight, seven,…." Kabir opened the door and Mr Prashant, the reporter, walked in.

Dr. Deshpandey has been arrested and sentenced imprisonment. He has been suspended from the hospital. Kabir was declared not guilty. Kanchan received her baby boy as Mrs Parker realised her mistake. They both share a strong bond of friendship now. Mrs Parker still considers Kanchan's baby as her own son. Maa and Papa are proud of me and Kabir. We are planning to get married next month.

Rohan Acharya

Rohan Acharya, final year engineering student from Nagpur, his hobbies include writing short poems, reading, film-making and playing cricket. Rohan likes keeping pace with current affairs and anything new on Social Media. In the past two years, he has extensively involved himself in making short films for cultural festival competitions in Central India colleges. In most of which he has fared well and received a positive response. Poetry writing has always been a constant companion/stress buster for Rohan.

A boy is losing faith in his life. He meets a girl who teaches him to live again. He starts to feel the joys of life in her presence. They become the best of friends. Slowly, they fall in love with each other. But somehow ,love leaves them with a lot of problems and one day after a bitter quarrel, the girl leaves the boy and unfortunately meets with an accident and dies. The boy, though, still believes, she's there with him. Sitting by her graveside, he remembers his past:

Silence

The days when I saw no light…
You had come somewhere close
You clenched my fist and we stormed the winds
And once again, the sun shone upon us

I started to dream more
I cared for the smiles now..
And the rains I started to feel
Walking all along, with you

I realized I belonged to you
Being your side, I won the world
There's nothing other I felt more
There's nothing other I needed more

But how do I beat this love
It came for us, and things changed…
Now, I no longer see you
Time has left me alone, all over again

I still roam the ways in the night
Hoping to find you somewhere
Humming a line, we would sing
Closing my eyes, I feel you near…

Someday again, we'll dare the rains
Laugh some more, dance once more
Someday again, I'll befriend my fate
Take you back and give away the silence…

Satyananda Sarangi

Satyananda Sarangi, a graduate in Electrical Engineering, is an emerging poet and fiction writer. A resident of the state of Odisha, India, he has more than seventy poems and a few short stories to his name. Apart from writing, he takes a keen interest in quizzing and the sport of cricket.

Recently, one of his short stories titled "The English Teacher" has been picked to feature in an upcoming book by Dream House Publications, India. In September 2015, his poem "More than Divine" was selected in the Delhi Poetry Challenge and published in "Kaafiyana" while another poem "A Handful Bliss" has been selected for another anthology. Earlier this year, four of his poems were also published in "Addiqtd Book of Poetry" (a joint venture of addiqtd.com and LJLF).

The Appalling Woods

The shadowy sunset looms up,
a tiresome day nearing its end,
is it some novelty in the air,
or worse mishaps that transcend?

Footmarks, footmarks all but muddy,
ahead of me, into the woods, they vanish,
as if of any human in peril,
sufficing to hum a tune so hellish.

What do I do at a time so odious?
my conscience is in a fix,
to go on or pull back,
my mind's in a state of transfix.

Years back, a myth had rumoured,
the woods were unsafe they said,
unfathomable, unknowable, far from their notion,
leaving many scared and the rest misled.

Locked in by the old age,
a withering physique gone frail,
my wit still very sound,
little courage put to good avail.

No dear ones, to shed tears,
no one to buy the shroud,
Into the woods, I must walk,

as the intrepid one from the crowd.

Stained By The Lily

A duty bound being craved once,
to escape the circles of duty,
I do recollect it is thou,
the one yearning for a diverse beauty.

Into deep delineations of the nature,
thy mood shall fly as a bird free,
away from the tedium, to somewhere,
to a land with tales quite eerie.

The white lily one of them,
all clothed in white and pious,
the spectacle that would hold thou,
easing thy journey so arduous.

It was profound beyond measure,
provoking an empty mind's thought,
never by any sagacious speech,
that depth it had taught.

Back home, thou found the traces of lily,
thy heart, the white traces had stained,
alas! these had slept for an age,
but are now miraculously awakened.

Forgotten

An ancient parable keeps sprouting,
little true and the rest made up,
an event of laughter for the sceptic,
though for others, an healing syrup.

Aeons after hearing so much,
I drop in at the silent dale quietly,
the remains of a broken house,
a sight disconcerting me greatly.

Querying they came, quite in number,
sons, wives, mothers and the others,
some eyes old, some young I saw,
down my spine, flowed a wave of shivers.

The bedlam among them so firm,
spoke of what they never knew,
all along only lending ears to tales,
as from infants to adults, they grew.

Behind the mountains, the sun hid,
darkness in me welcomed the outer one,
I was their hero, it was my land I knew,
only pity, I was the only one.

Dr Waseem Malla

Dr Waseem A Malla, a Veterinarian by qualification and a Molecular Biologist by specialisation, belongs to a small hamlet in the Paradise on Earth - Kashmir. He is a 23 year old trilingual writer of prose and poems, a lazy blogger and an occasional book reviewer. He began writing a few years ago in English, but now dedicates most of his time to Urdu poetry that has always been his first love and his only inspiration, in addition to his mother tongue, Kashmiri. His poems have been published in a number of anthologies and journals in India and abroad alongside literary stalwarts. One of his poems is a part of a novel by a Canadian author. His favourites include Mirza Asadullah Khan Ghalib, Ahmad Faraaz, Agha Shahid Ali, Parveen Shakir, Orhan Pamuk, Elif Shafak and Fyodor Dostoevsky.

Madman's Utterances

Your memories bloom like Roses in spring,
Salt in my tears as their soil to grow,
I sit by a window of my exiled hut,
Contemplating; to find that long lost solace.

On a wheel I spin loss and loneliness,
Sorting apart threads of immortality and life,
From those of being and not being at all,
To draw colored ones - anew- of shades numerous!

Thousands of thoughts tread on paths in mind:
I breath, count me among those alive!
Bury me in earth's lap, I feel numb!
Breathe- you life? Numbness- You death? Oh, I wonder!

Let me be damned to fierce fire of Hell,
I'm not an angel - nay - for I've sinned!
Condemn me to the bliss of Heaven, Oh!
I'm not a devil - nay - for I've virtues.

Why is the Moon shrouded black, not white,
And what should I do to cremate the Fire?
Where does the Sun find a lamp for its house,
And who waters the Sea to quench its thirst?

I stand puzzled and my thoughts unmasked,
Words fly back to fetch me a title- Madman!

Wild Guesses

The sun sets somewhere far away,
Lands where angels and nymphs reside;

The evening sky dresses itself bridal,
In its rosy red gown- Ah, so sublime!

Who by this hour captivates my soul,
Illuminating lamps of false hope- dreams-
In the barren courtyard of imagination?

Memories of whose touch kill my pain?
Ah, so wonderfully peeping into my head!

Dreams - shattered- shared with whom,
Prick my eyes to weep red and salt?

What strange pains strangle my heart,
Or what insanity entangles me, to be damned?

What golden secrets I crave to bargain for dust,
And which buyer - I wait for - to own me?

I check my thoughts and turn to seek-
But aloof I stand, with no one around!

If she loved too, why does she still live,
And death be not her master in every breath?

Why the gazelle's eyes bear pearls of wisdom,
When love is nought but intoxicated sanity?

I wonder if she has waited all along- gazing-
Her eyes turned rock solid on my path!

But this I know, with no speck of doubt,
A mad, haunted me is making guesses, so wild!

Susmit Sarkar

Susmit Sarkar is a currently a 4th year Electrical Engineering student at Netaji Subhash Engineering College, Kolkata, India. He is an internationally published author too. His debut novel is titled "THE COALFIELD EXPRESS... The Thrill is about to Begin" with Partridge Publishers, a Penguin Random House. The book is available at Amazon worldwide. Apart from that he is a lyricist and compose a variety of songs in English, Hindi and Bengali. He has also been short listed for an upcoming anthology title 'Paper Boat' by Dream House Publication, India. He resides at Durgapur, a city you can easily pinpoint on the map of West Bengal, India. He can be easily reached at s.susmit11@gmail.com

A Morning Walk...
...Through the Grass of Destiny

Thirteen, a combination of two such numerical digits which when left alone do not pose any threat to the superstitions of Human Intellect. But once they combine together, even a harmless sneeze through the breeze of a cold weather gives it the tagline of being "The Unlucky 13". But today I am going to change that... atleast give it my best shot.

The calendar goes back to the date of 10th March with the year 2007 printed in bold letters. Standing in front of it, Rik took his sharpened pencil and marked it in a circle, after all, how many vacations does one get to spend in peace. The final examination of class 7 has just taken its farewell leaving the countless days of misery far behind for him. And now its time for his league of games to begin. But what about the date? Well if you ask me, that's the date when the digits of unlucky thirteen have just started to show off its colours in the characteristics of this 13-year-old teenager. If you start chiseling out his character sketch, there won't be a single piece of unique art effect you can boast of, but I am pretty sure that there will be a lot of flaws not even a single parent would dare to approve of. Laziness, pessimistic, selfish, you name it and it will be there in him. It has been almost two years since he had stepped in at St. Xavier's and yet his dark phases have not yet burned in its furnace. What was destiny waiting for? I don't know but maybe for a day coming soon. "What? This can't happen. How can it happen that we didn't get tickets to Delhi?", began the frustration of the thirteen-year-old teenager. "Well that's because you changed the destination at the last point and by that time all the seats got reserved", replied the patience of his father. "Damn it", spoke up Rik to let out his disappointment take the form of his words. "Stupid, isn't it father? I am really stupid", replied his words. Out of all the darkness, his readiness to accept his fault seemed like the only silver lining of his character. "Told you we wouldn't get the tickets at the last moment. You only chose to differ", added Rik's mother, as she came out of the kitchen holding a tray with Rik's favourite delicacies spread out across its palate. "So we don't get to go anywhere this vacation, isn't it?", asked Rik's words with the hope that his father would suddenly surprise him with the tickets to Delhi. But that was never to happen. "Yes it does seem like that", Mr. Sarkar's words seemed to drill in the final nail in the coffin of his son's hope. "Unless you choose another destination", Mrs. Sarkar's seemed to rejuvenate her son's hope contrary to his father. "And where would that be?", questioned Rik's words as his crooked eyebrows emphasized on how hard his neurons were trying to guess the answer. "Bandel", replied his mother. "Trust me even a great painter would find himself short of colours to paint out its beauty", added her words. "No way, that's a barren land devoid of any scenic beauty", shot back Rik. Mrs. Sarkar heavy sigh showed that she had already anticipated the answer, just as she had uttered the name of her maternal place. Seeing the complexity of the situation, Mr. Sarkar decide to take the decision. "I am pretty sure there will be some areas which are still awaiting the presence of your feet. Have a nice trip." Even before the spark of revolt could afford to arise, the case was shut and dismissed.

By next morning, their feet succeeded in landing at their destination Sahaganj, Bandel. All thanks to the Mayurakshi Fast Passenger Train takes just two hours in accomplishing the measured distance of 131 km. As the doorbell rang, the door opened to unleash the 5.5 feet gentleman like figure that stood there to welcome his grandson and daughter. Even at the age of 60, his stout figure could leave any human intellect baffled about his personality. That was Rik's grandfather. "Welcome Rik, welcome to your grandfather's humble abode", spoke out his voice with the entire warmth enveloped in its leaves. A smile sketched itself across Rik's lips as his eyes met with that of his ancestor. "It had been almost a year since we last met, isn't it Grandfather?", spoke his words as Rik bent down to touch his feet following the custom of our very own Indian Culture. "Indeed Rik, I have been waiting for you pretty long enough". With that, Rik entered the abode which was humble only in words but seemed pretty rich in his vision. The entire day went off in some chit chats ranging from Examination Results to the future planning. Rik's enthusiasm seemed to come down with the passage of each hour as the elderly lectures stormed down at him, completely unaware that the next day would reveal in the path of his destiny. The night had already pulled down its curtain gathering the darkest of the shadows from all sides. Dinner was over and the hour hand at eleven along with all its silence signified that the entire family had gone to sleep. Its just the dim light of the veranda that peeked into Rik's eyeliner to suggest him that his grandfather was upto something. As his steps closed in, he could see that his grandfather was putting in the lace through the maze of those countless holes in his sports shoe. "What are you doing Grandfather?", asked Rik's voice. "Nothing much Rik, just preparing my kit for tomorrow's morning walk", came down his reply. "From when did you start taking a morning walk?", arrowed another question from the grandson. "A lot of things have changed in the past one year. Seems like you have missed a lot of its fun", chuckled the voice in reply. Unable to hide his eagerness, Rik spoke up, "Can I come too?" "Of course, let's take a trip".

Rik never had the luxury of getting up late by the clock, thanks to his early morning school at 7:30 am. So getting up early was not a problem. As he tied up his shoe lace, the duo took off for a morning walk. Mr. Dutta, well that's the honourable title of Rik's grandfather, strapped the watch across his wrist which showed the time as 6:00 am. The vague layers of a slight fog adorned the path of their morning walk. May not be as clear as a crystal, but the roads were still under the decent range of visibility. They wrapped up their hooded jackets and started off with a light jogging. "So how is History doing?", asked Mr. Dutta as if History was a person with a human form. "Not good, fell ill and had quite a high fever during the examinations, you know", shot back the grandson with the same proforma in mind. "I see, didn't you give it proper medicine?", asked Mr. Dutta,

110

resembling the pattern they were used to. As the subjects took the human form in Rik's childhood, they have continued to be so in his teenage. "Still fighting against the British to achieve its freedom", carried on Rik's words, "I don't know why the Indians allowed them to step onto our land? It would have saved us not only a fortune but also a great burden of the syllabus. From the pages of History, it seems like they came down to India just wage wars against us. Didn't they have any other work?", questioned Rik's disgust against the whole lot of syllabus ranging from the first war of Independence to its last. "Do you know what I think? It seems like you have turned upon the dark pages only and that's the reason why you have fallen at the wrong footnote", replied his grandfather's patience. "In the entire syllabus of history, there is not even a single syllable that calls in for a praise for the British. They did nothing for India", spoke out Rik's disgust. "In that case, let me have the pleasure of showing you something that your intellect can use in favour of the British, at least, you could stop hating them". With that, the smooth road took a right turn along its way.

"In this city? Are you kidding? Except for the Bandel Church built by the Portuguese, there is nothing this city is famous of", chuckled Rik's voice as his jogging reduced to a light morning walk. "May not be 'is', but what if 'was'?", their eyes met, Rik trying his best to read the thoughts scribbled on his grandfather's forehead, which contained a lot of criss-cross lines sketched on its palate. Both their feet stopped. "What happened? Why did we stop here?", questioned Rik, as he realized that the path they had taken was not a familiar one. "That's because we have reached our destination", Mr. Dutta's hands resembling his words showed the way. In front of them stood a seemingly thousand-year-old gate with the creepers flowering out its greenery across its bars. "What is this place Grandfather?", asked the grandson, as Mr. Dutta opened the gates to reveal a place which seemed deserted long ago. "Told you, you have not flipped all the pages of History", whispered Mr.Dutta's voice into Rik's ears. Their steps took them inside, as the shiny droplets on the grass leaflets greeted them with the same enthusiasm as had when the Britishers had first stepped inside. "This is the compound of one of the most reputed tyre manufacturing companies that used to be flourishing on the map of India", said Mr. Dutta. "And what was its name?", asked the little historian's curiosity. "The Dunlop Rubber Company India Ltd., Sahaganj", seemed like Rik has just entered a new arena of History.

As they continued their journey, the morning walk took them through a new timeline about which Rik has never heard of before. "Tell me more about this place grandfather." "It seems like history has started to sketch out a different character in your mind", smiled Mr. Dutta as he could see Rik's perspective change for the better. "Well the Britishers not only got themselves busy in waging wars, they did have the luxury of redefining the cities too. And this is one of its examples", continued Mr. Dutta's words as their steps took them forward. "There was a man named John Boyad Dunlop, who went on to discover pneumatic tyres. He was the man who started the Dunlop Rubber Company and that's the company which started the manufacture of cycle tyres in India in the year of 1896. In the year 1936, Dunlop set up its first tyre manufacturing unit in Asia on a 239-acre plot of land", continued his words, "And do you know which place was it?" "Which one grandfather?" "The same place you are standing upon right now, Sahaganj", concluded the wise words. "Tyres? That does not seem difficult. Its nothing but a circular piece of rubber with an inflated tube inside", spoke up Rik. "Trust me when I say this, Rik. It's a way more than just that. It's the tyre manufacturers because of whose skills the modern day road transport has taken its shape of what it is today. Its not just the air-filled pneumatic tyres that Dunlop had authority upon. They manufactured OTR tyres or in other words 'OFF THE ROAD' tyres because of which your father's car gets a strong hold of those rough terrains", explained the wise words. By now Rik was completely out of his wit. "Do you see that? That used to be one of the cleanest hospital people used to depend upon on those days", as Mr. Dutta's raised finger showed Rik the remains of the building, as a brick crumbled down from its torso. "And that was a fire brigade station which housed three fire engines at a time", the deserted hall seemed large enough to hold even four engines at a time. "Well now it seems like they had worked other than waging war too", Rik was turning the unknown pages of History. "But grandfather did they manufacture just tyres for cycle?", questioned Rik. "No dear, they were far ahead of time. With added capabilities, they mastered a lot of tricks. As time passed, they started manufacturing tyres for cars, trucks and even tractors.

The actual revolution came in when they started manufacturing tyres for aircrafts. That was the year of 1942 when the world was moving towards the end of the Second World War", concluded Mr. Dutta's words.

"So what about History now, Rik?", questioned Mr. Dutta. "Well, right now History is feeling as healthy as a horse", replied Rik. "Do you know what my watch is telling me?" "What grandfather?" "That its time for us to return. I am pretty sure you don't a search squad after us", chuckled Mr. Dutta's word, "The rest of the history can be completed later." With that, they started retracing their path back to their heavenly abode, in short their home. "Thank you, grandfather, you have changed my perspective about History completely. From now on History will never be a burden, it will be taking its morning walk everyday with me just by my side", conveyed the words of Rik's heart. "I hope so, dear. It seems like your dark characters have started burning in the furnace of History to reveal the colour of gold hidden inside you", replied the wise words of his grandfather in return, completely unaware that one day his grandson would scribble down his words in the pages of history for the world to know about the place called 'Sahaganj'.

The Adrenaline Crush...

She ran as fast as she could. Not on the stairs but on the infinite railway tracks that lay ahead of her. Clad in those blade scratched jeans, she jumped over to take down the obstacle that she had stumbled over a year ago. A year ago she could barely run without getting caught by the monster, always behind her back. But now she not only ran, but ran fast enough to leave her monsters far behind. Her thundering steps took her straight up the inclined board. Granules of those minute sand particles were scattered here and there up the pathway when suddenly she found herself running desperately on the top of those rusty railway coaches. She jumped to clear the gap and step down on the successive coaches one after the other. Her jumping shoes took her back on the railway tracks. With her unbeatable speed, she was no less than Ussain Bolt at the moment. In an attempt to jump over another rock, she missed the signal which had turned its camouflage colour back to green. She heard it or not, but was definitely under panic attack when for once she looked back to find the gigantic machine emerge from the shadows. Shadows of the tunnel she had crossed just a few seconds ago. She ran as fast as she could but she was not fast enough to escape the collision or I should say the fate of death she was about to meet.

And Bang! The entire screen of her brand new smartphone got blank with the words GAME OVER flashing all over. The score that flashed was enough to designate her as the new record holder of the so-called game 'Subway Surfer'. She definitely didn't escape the collision even in the real world, when her shoulder accidentally brushed that of the boy her fluttering hair encountered on her way out. "Sorry", said the thick-spectacled boy who had taken his first step on his first day into the engineering college. But she barely noticed his benign words. It wouldn't have mattered to him much, had he not fallen for her jet black eyes, with her rose coloured lips completing his fantasy. He was about to fall into his first crush, had it not been for the blaring noise that tried its best to distract his thoughts. He looked at her once more. "Must be a senior", said his barely audible whisper. "Or maybe a first year", rejoiced his thoughts. But whatever it was, her fantasies was definitely not going to spare him the sparks of anger he was about to face being so late for his first class.

"May I come in Sir?", this time, he seemed more benign than the last time 'Sorry'. Still thinking who that 'he' was. For those who haven't guessed it yet, well it was me, me with the name Arnav Srikanth hanging down my I-Card. "I wish you could. But it seems like you are too early for your next class", came a stern reply straight out of the blue. I looked at my watch and realized the meaning of his words. The hour hand ticked the clock at 10:00 am. In short, I was 30 minutes late for my Chemistry class and 30 minutes early for my Maths class. The door was shut on my face. I turned around to find an empty corridor staring back at the sole pedestrian waiting to take a walk. Hardly did I have any option but to idle away the time in taking a quick glimpse of the other Departments in the college. After all, you got to spend the next four years in that arena. 30 minutes passed by in a jiffy. The door finally opened. The Chemistry professor came out with a bunch of followers having infinite doubts still hovering above their heads. They definitely didn't want to miss those unknown links in their chemical bonds. I went inside to find an empty first bench near the window, opened it and took a deep breath to feel a new atmosphere. Losing my bag, I sat down and looked around only to realize that I was the only one left in the class. "Isn't this class scheduled for Maths?", I asked the last one that was about to leave too. "Seems like you didn't get a chance to stumble upon the new routine. It has been changed to Electrical Machines Lab, my friend." Really! First the Chemistry class and now this. What is happening with me! To avoid being thrown out again, I rushed behind my still unknown classmates. Taking the steps down the hall, I reached the Machine's Lab. I was definitely the last one to step inside, when suddenly I wasn't. "May I come in Sir?", spoke out hers' and my voice together. The same jet black eyes and the fluttering hair with a fringe coming down her forehead took my heartbeats to a new level. Damn, she was beautiful. "Oh yes, do come in", said the lab assistant. She rushed to collect the lab manual. I didn't. I have still not been able to contain my heartbeats within myself. So she is indeed the first year. I don't know whether fortunately or unfortunately, as we were the last to enter, we managed to combine ourselves into the last group with the Thevenin's Theorem experiment sheet fluttering in her hands. Gone, gone, gone both my heart as well as my first lab experiment, thought my heartbeats. She looked at me to have a glimpse of her new lab partner, who was definitely out of her league. "Do you have any idea of how to do it?", asked her words. "French Kiss or Indian?", I wanted to ask, with her rose lips still blushing as before. "Hello, I asked you something", she asked again. "Oh yes", replied my words, taking a break from my daydreams. I looked at the circuit board, just to realize that the answer should have been a 'NO'. The rest of the students hardly had any idea. So any help was certainly uncertain. "So lets start. You need to make the connections, take the reading and get the results checked", instructed her words. "Really! And what do you intend to do?", I asked. "Sit around here and watch you do it", she shot back. I could hardly resist my smile. "So what do we start with?", she asked. "With wires maybe", I said and went to bring some connecting wires from the wire section. "Are you sure you know Thevenin's Theorem?", asked the lab assistant, seeing how eager I was to complete it. I blurted out the only thing I had fortunately read the last night, the official statement of the Thevenin's Theorem. 'She' was definitely impressed. Seemed like I have scored my marks with the introductory chapter. I started fiddling with the wires, making many wrong connections as possible. The impression quotient got lesser and lesser as far as the lab assistant is concerned unless there was a sudden spark. She had accidentally switched on the main switch. We had nothing but burnt copper wires in our hands. Within seconds, we found ourselves standing outside the Principal's office.

"Sorry Sir", screamed our words out. "I know you are. But what I want is not a SORRY but a reason not to suspend both of you. Do you have one?", asked his rough voice. We stood there mum. "Come on, give me something at least. Whose fault was it?", this time his voice rougher. "Mine", I blurted out even before she could say something. She looked at me as if she couldn't believe her ears. "Good then, you get suspended on your first day itself", said the Principal. "No Sir, it was my fault", spoke her words. And this time, I couldn't believe my ears. Our eyes met and time stood standstill for a moment. Mr.Principal cleared his throat to break the cosmic connection we were about to feel for each other. Who had a crush on whom? Even I didn't know, but the cupid's arrow had struck the right chords with both of us. "I liked the fact that both of you turned out to be honest. But trust me, this is the first and the last time you are leaving my office unharmed. Next time be aware", said those rough words again. With that, we left. "Why did you take up the colour of blame yourself?", she asked. "To fall in love with you", I wanted to say. But my words chose to be different. "Maybe because I didn't want you to get suspended on the first day of your college or maybe because I wanted to win the beats of your heart", I said as if I was not serious. A curvy smile did appear across her lips. "Not a bad way to make friends, huh", she said. "Yes, but we could have started off on a better note", I replied back "And what's that?", she was damn curious. "With your name, maybe", I said.

"Oh yes. My name is Avantika. And yours?" "Arnav", I replied back.

Time passed away like the wind and except for that sole encounter, we hardly ever talked. Facebook, Whats App, Twitter, Instagram, you name it and she will be there. Its just me who had beenn't. Facebook was the first platform I had the fortune to step upon. Incessant texting was not something I was accustomed to until I managed to come across her profile. I used to linger to the 15-inch screen of my laptop, just to have a glimpse of her profile picture. Hardly did I have the courage to chat with her. What would I start with? Hello? Hi? How are you? Unable to decide, I used to log out most of the times. I didn't want to become a stalker. You know the word Voyeurism was never my type. Finally, I mustered all the strength I had and hit the send button with the word HELLO in bold letters. One minute passed away. Another 30 seconds passed away. I did have an adrenaline rush or better to say an Adrenaline Crush, my heartbeats increasing with each passing second. "Hello", came back the reply. Seemed like I had won a war. After that what took place was a complete one hour of incessant texting. By now we knew a lot of things about each other, except the fact of whether we were single or not. So I asked first. "Are you ready to mingle?", asked my quirky words. "Only if my heart was single", replied her truthful words. "Great", I replied, trying to hide the cracks of my broken heart as far as possible. "And who is that lucky guy?", I typed the letters with tears in my eyes. "Can't reveal right now. Would meet him tomorrow when we meet for our first date.", replied her comment. "Enjoy the blissful moments with him". The tear that had been lingering so far on the edge fell on the keyboard as I clicked the Enter button. In 22 years of my life, I had fallen for one, only to realize that she could have never been mine.

Leaving her thoughts far behind, I jumped. Not from the highest building in the arena, but from the platform I had been running onto. I ran through those infinite stone slabs that made up the railway tracks. I wanted to die but couldn't stop running. I jumped over the obstacles. My jumping shoes took me straight ahead. And whenever I saw some train coming towards me I changed my track. But what I was running out of, was my charge, my life force, when suddenly someone swiped the screen and the words "GAME OVER" emerged in bold letters. "What the hell?", I screamed out and turned around only to find Avantika's eyes piercing straight through my heart. "Sorry, but you were pretty close in breaking my record of the so-called game Subway Surfer", said her words. "What are you doing here? Shouldn't you be with your date right now?", I asked completely puzzled. "I am, Arnav. Its just that you haven't realised it yet", replied her words. "Seems like you are not the only one who had succumbed to the Adrenaline Crush", added her words. I couldn't stop smiling and neither could she. "You are indeed a great teaser Avantika", I said as she sat down beside me to give me the best company I could have ever imagined.

www.ingramcontent.com/pod-product-compliance
Lightning Source LLC
Chambersburg PA
CBHW070755120626
46557CB00002B/609